Coloring book for adults and kids monkey image for design

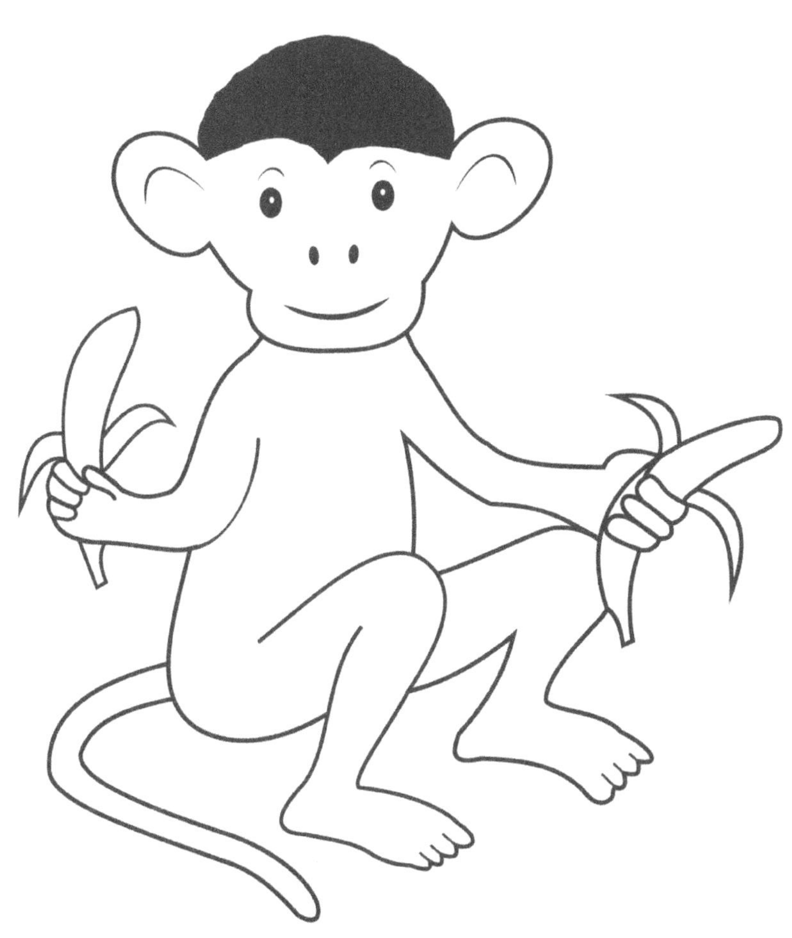

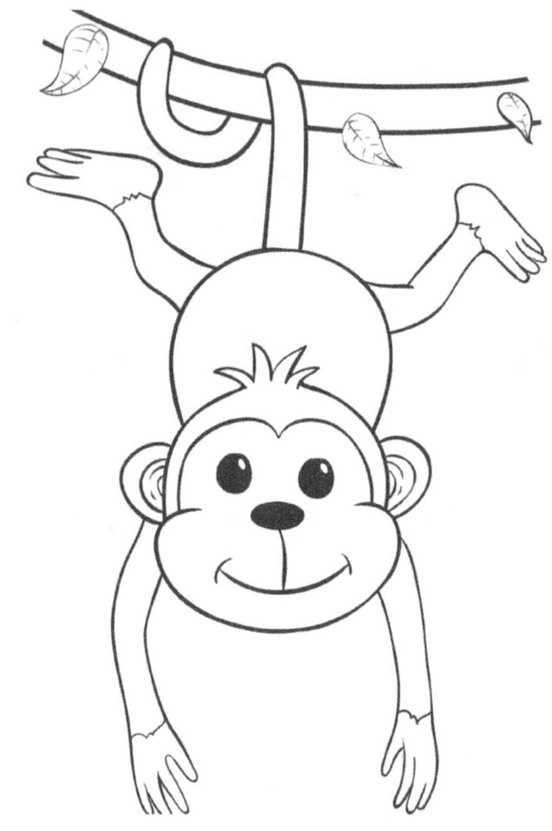

This coloring book is belongs to

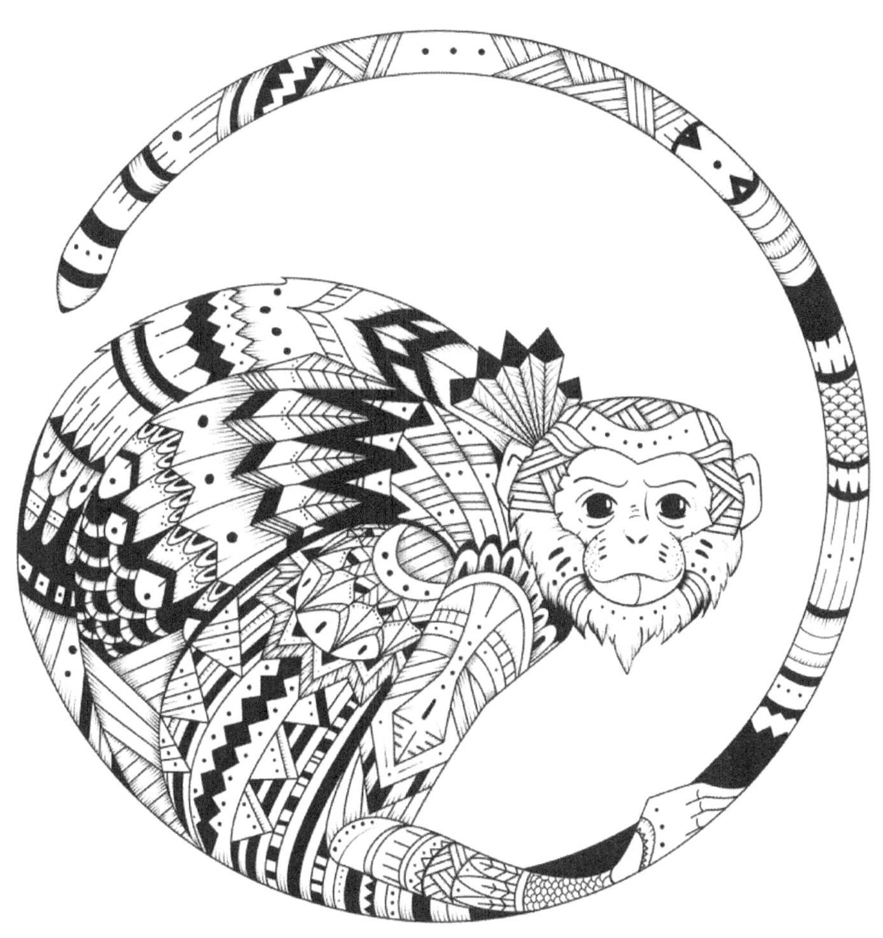

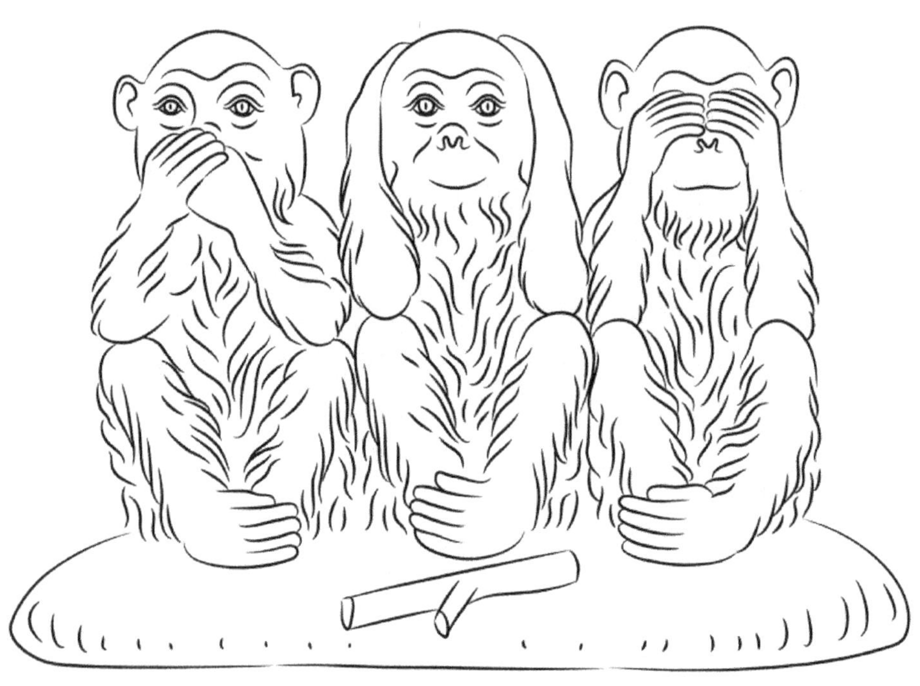

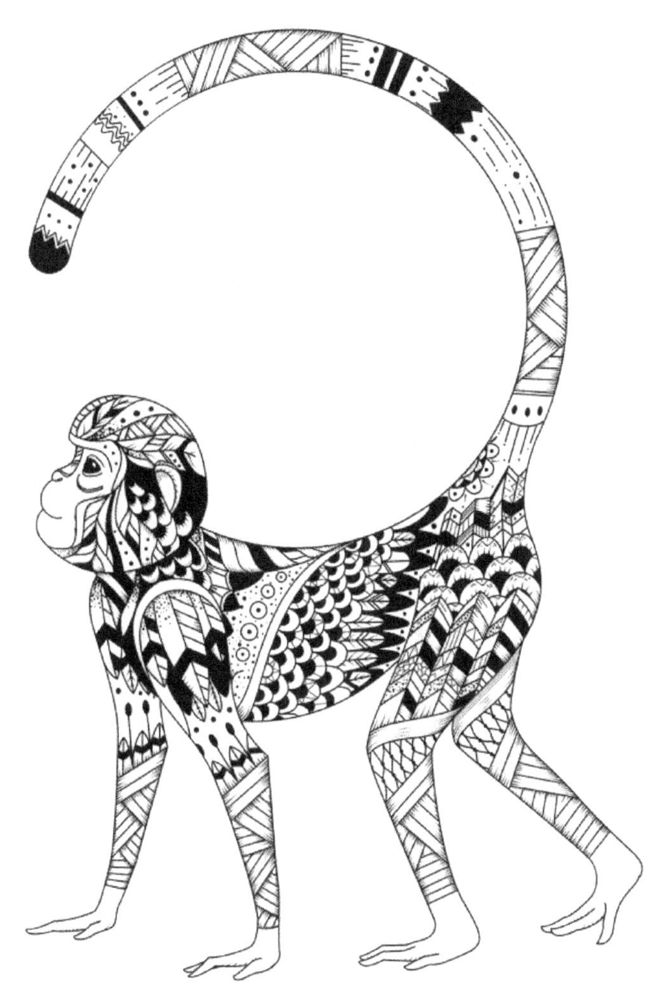

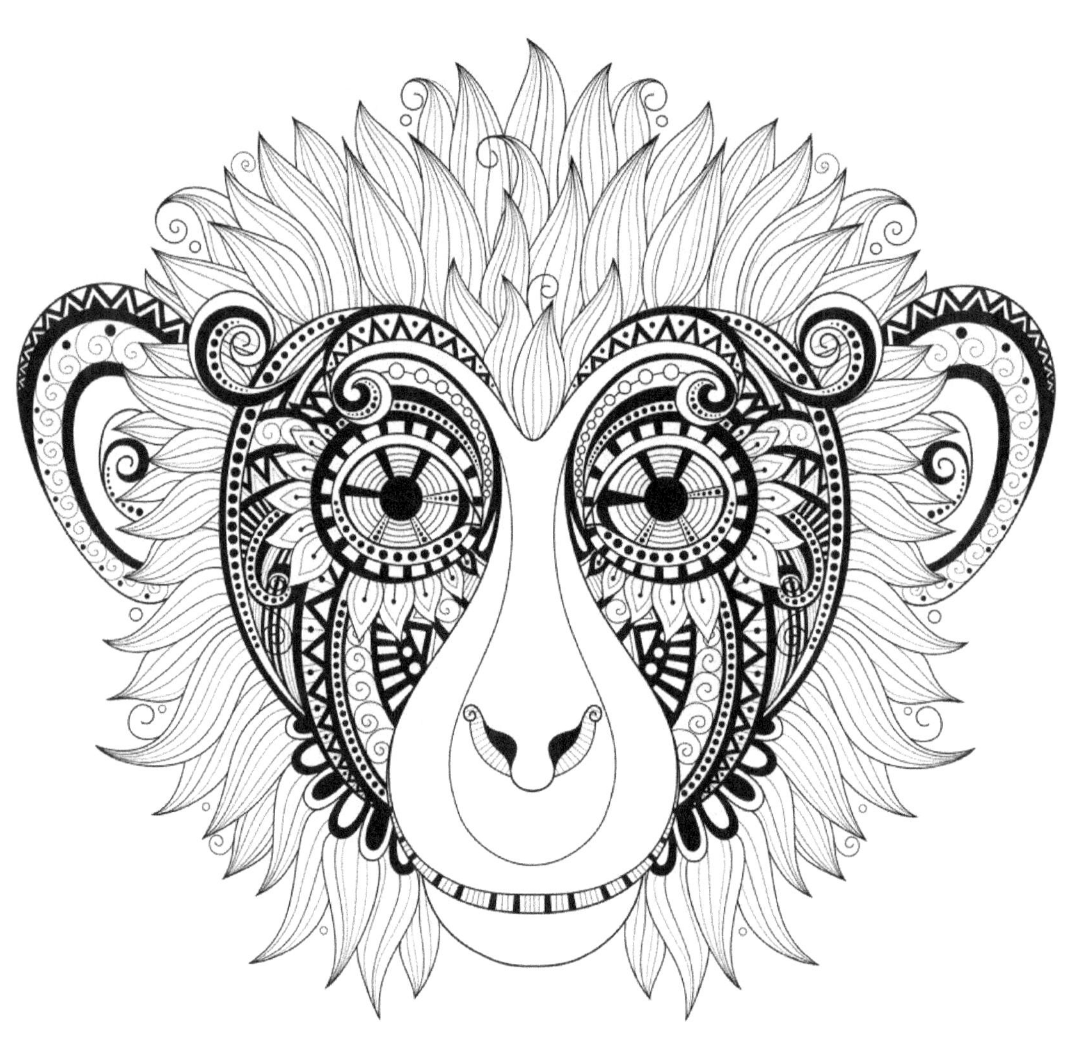

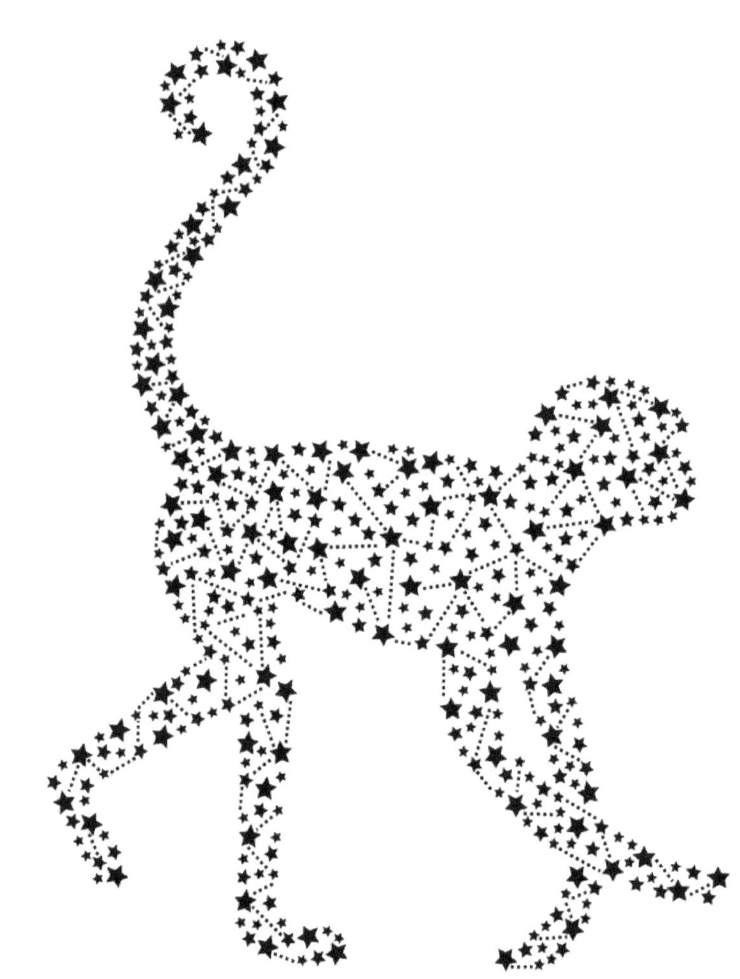

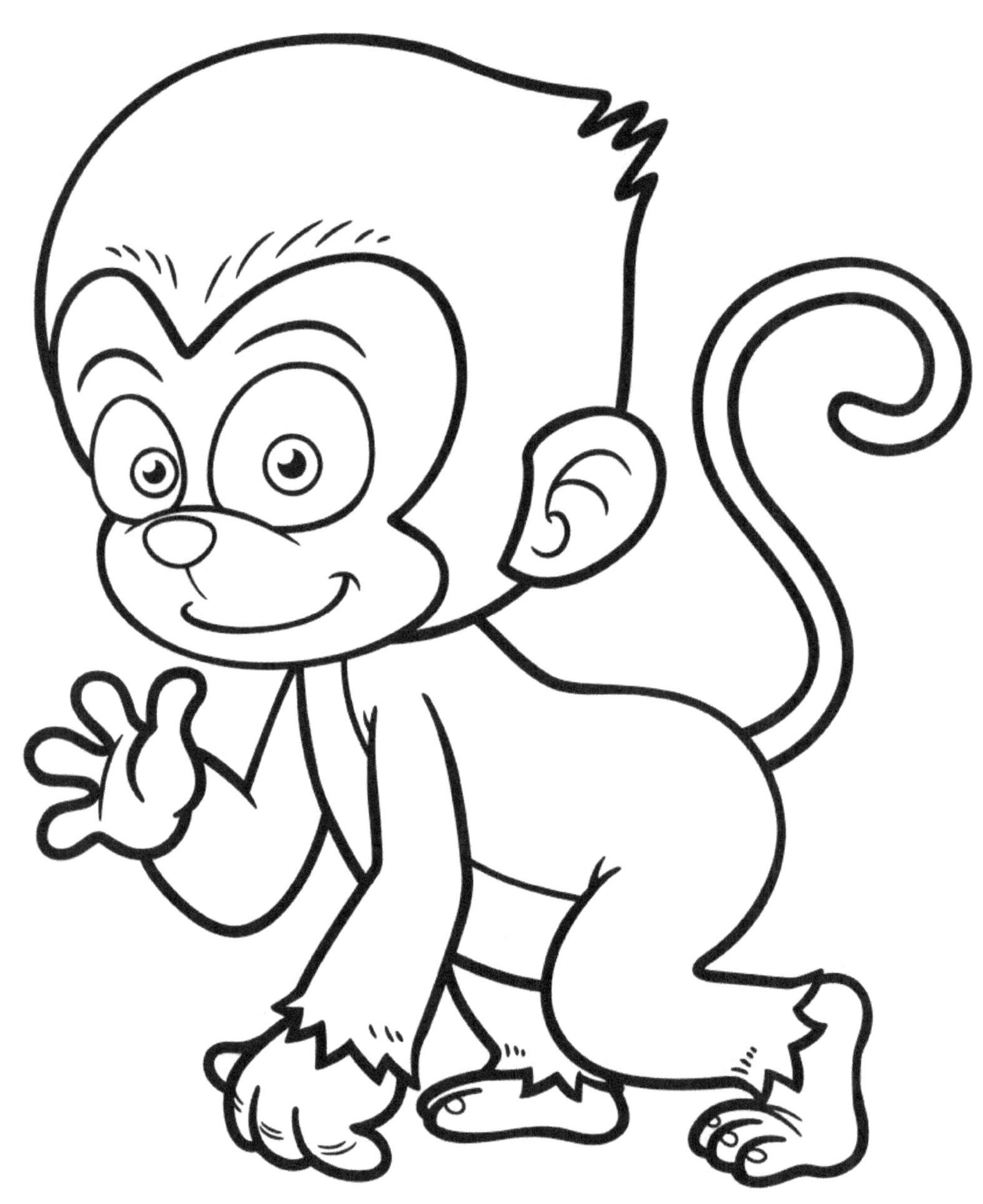

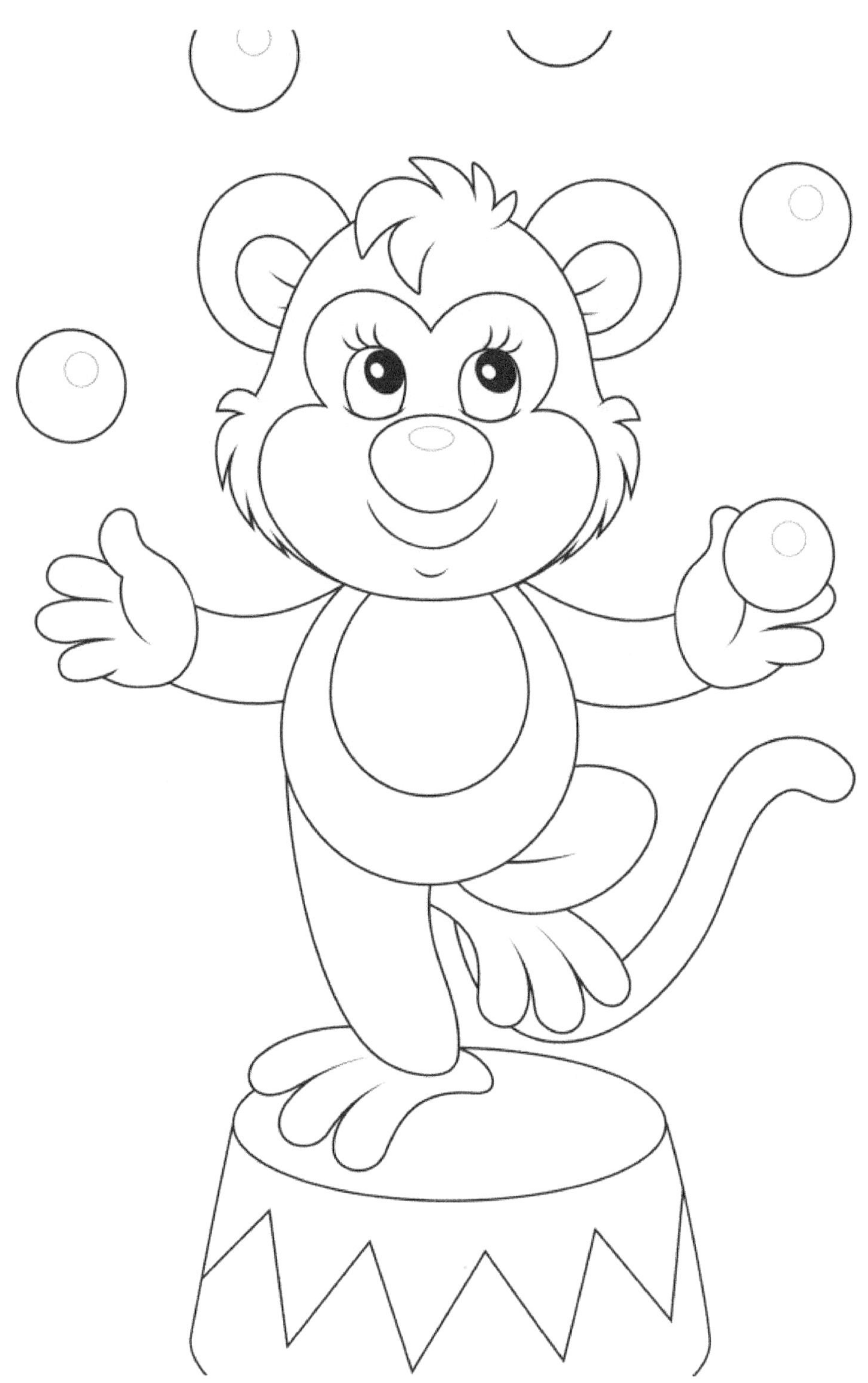

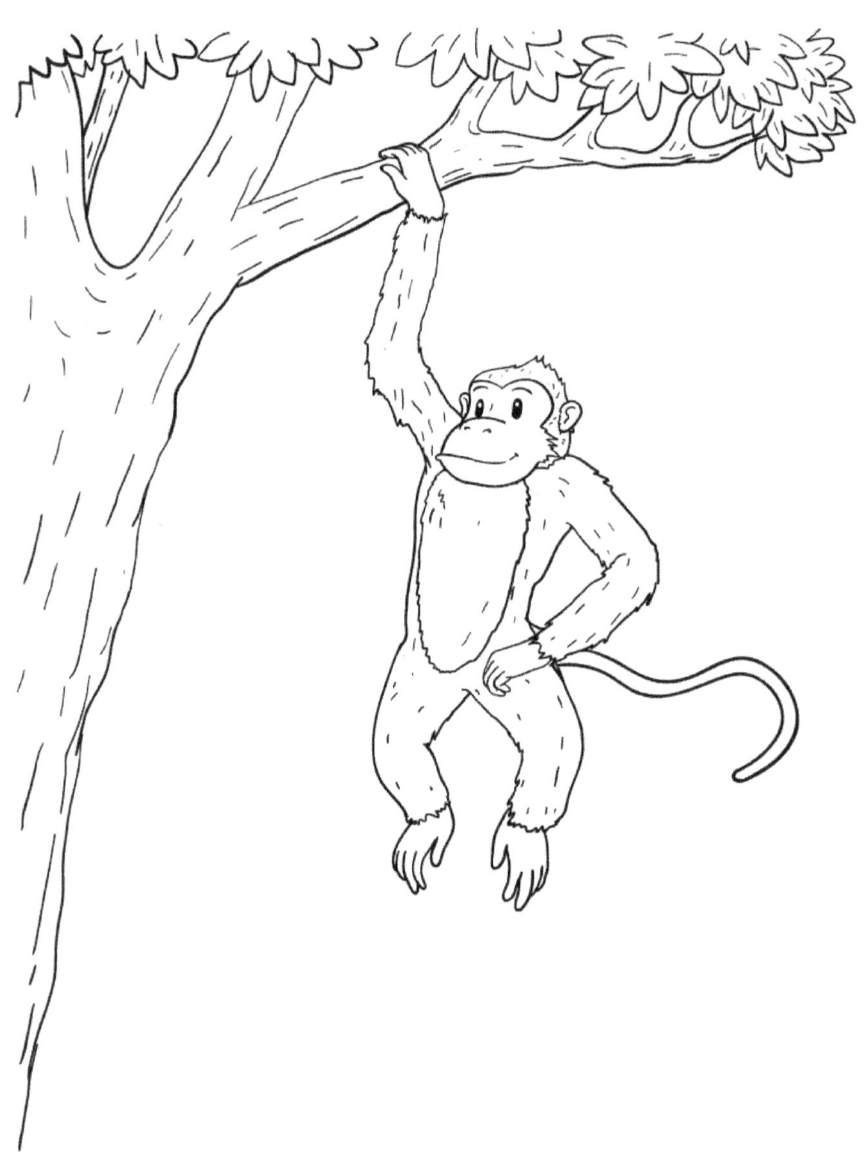

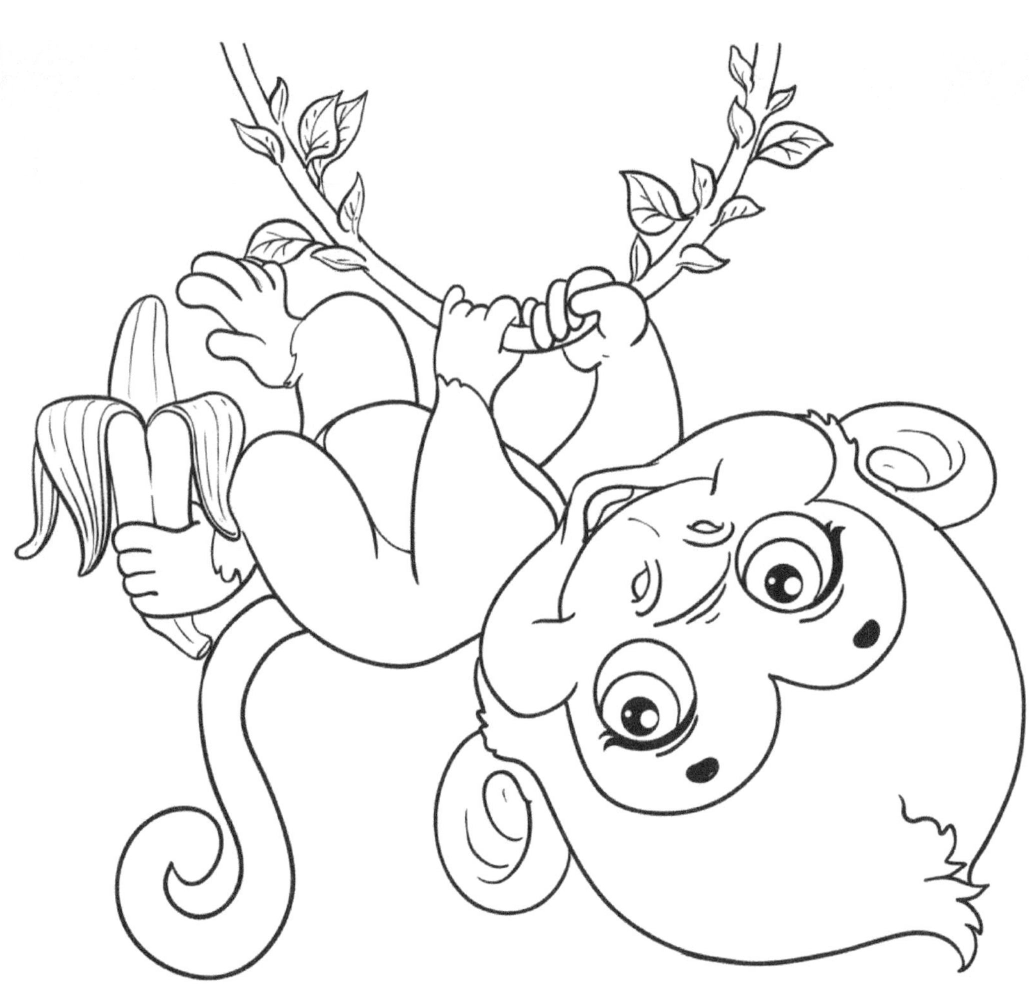

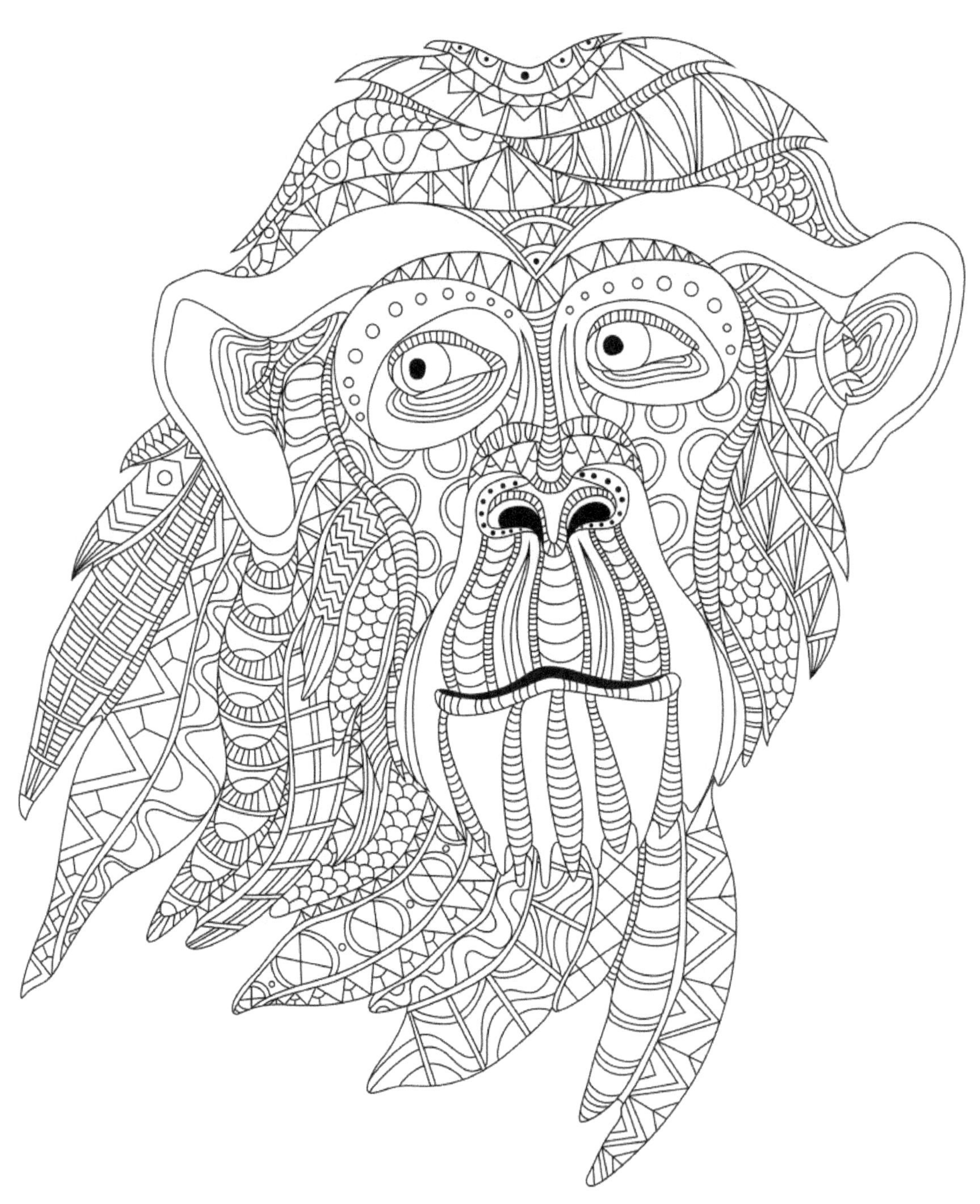

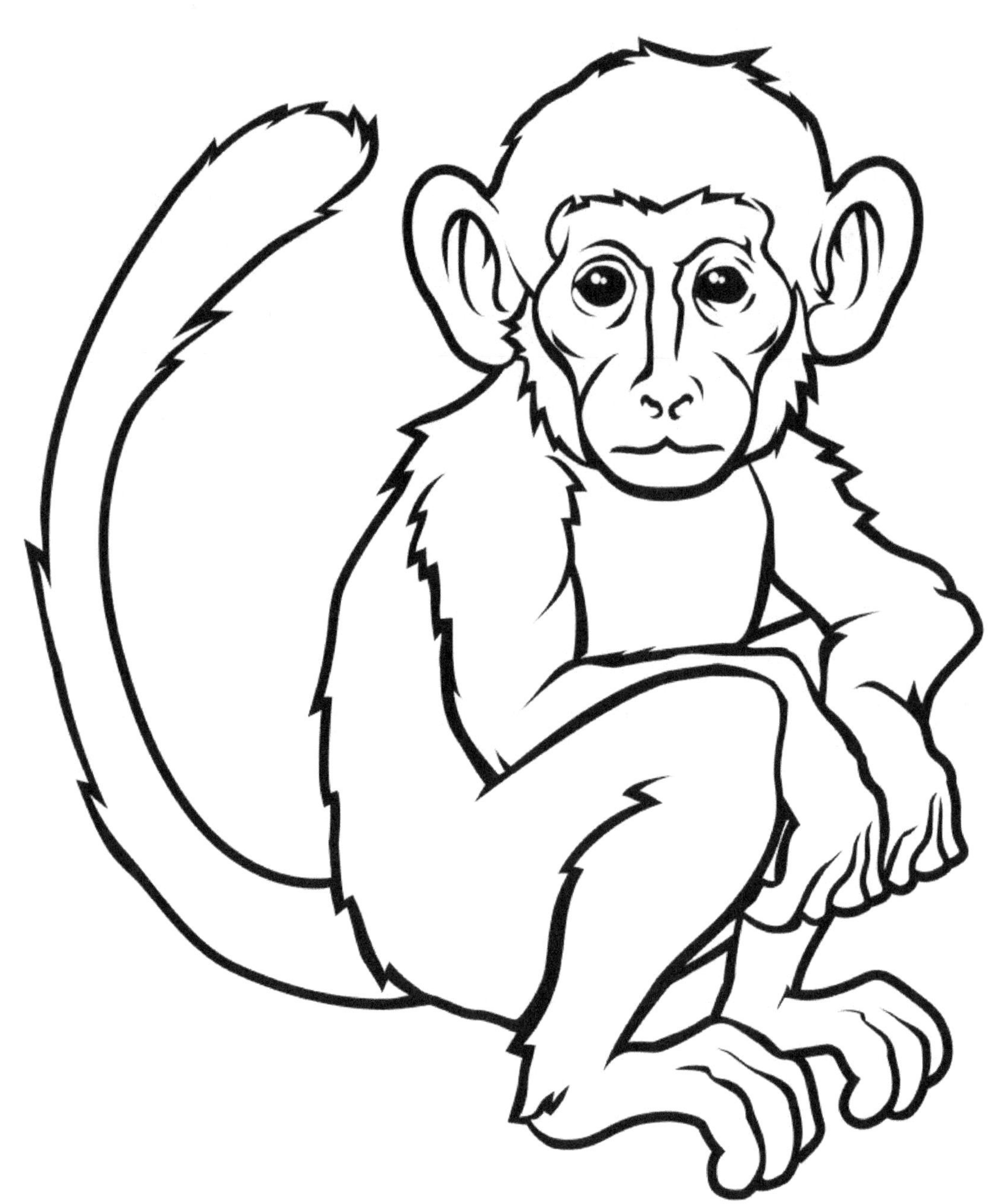

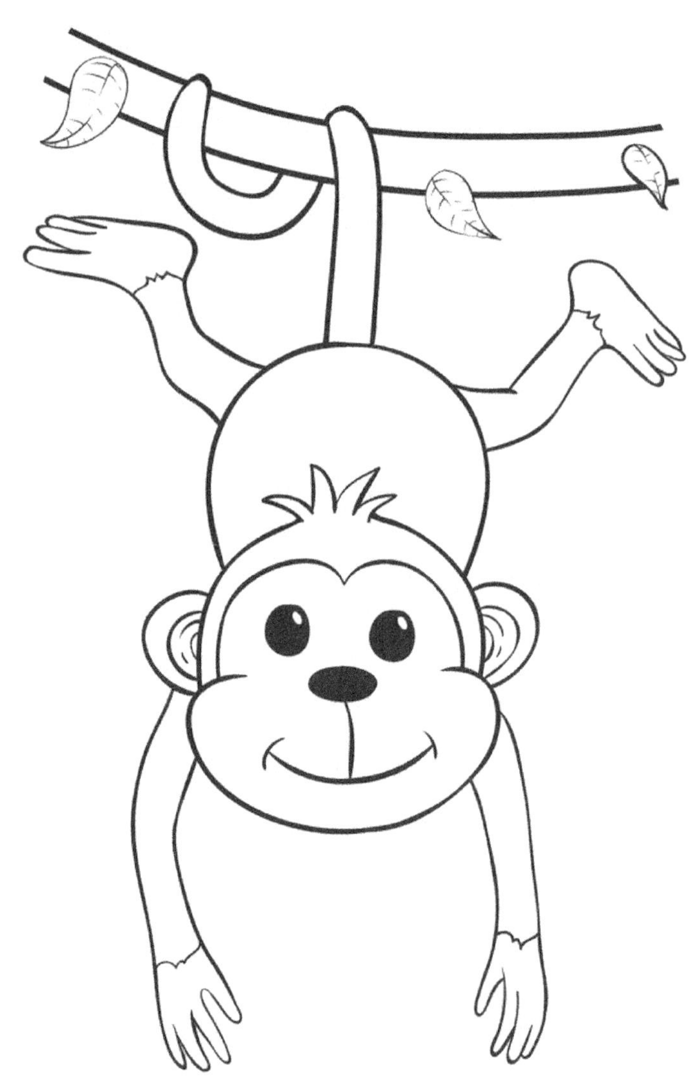

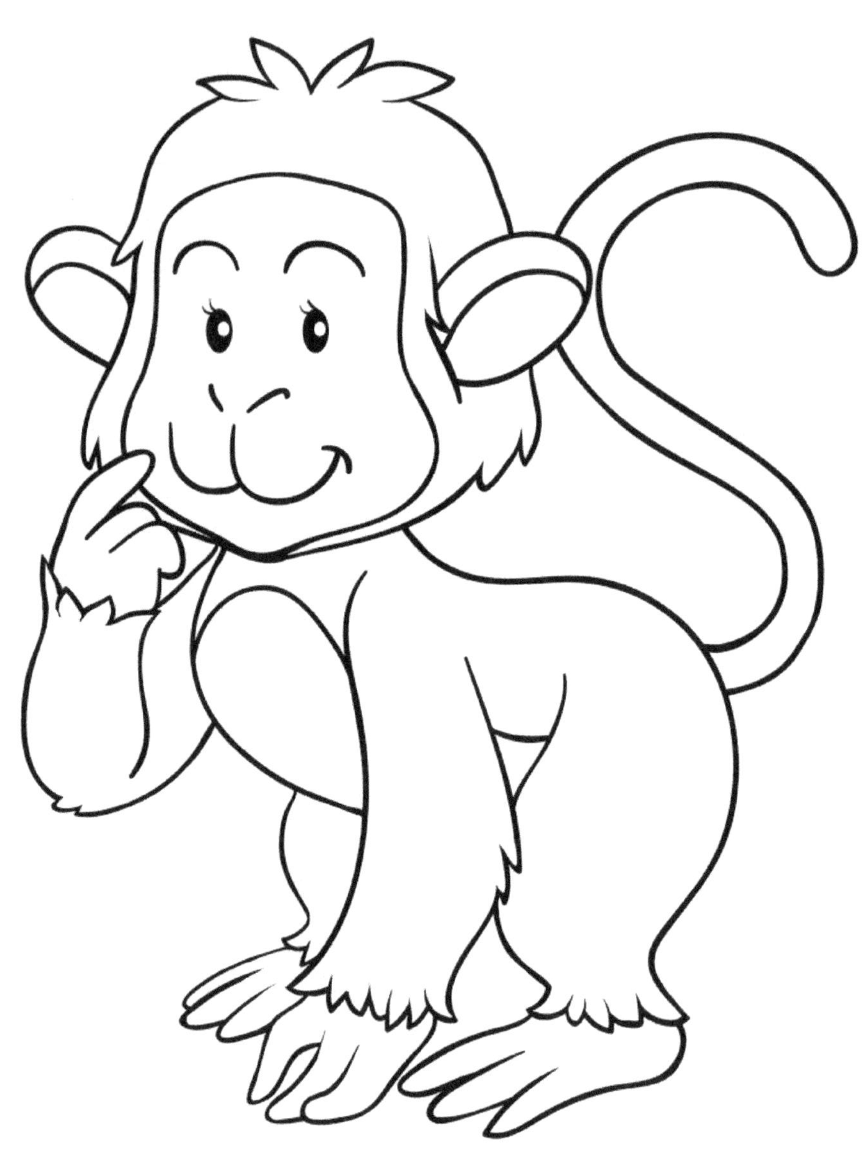

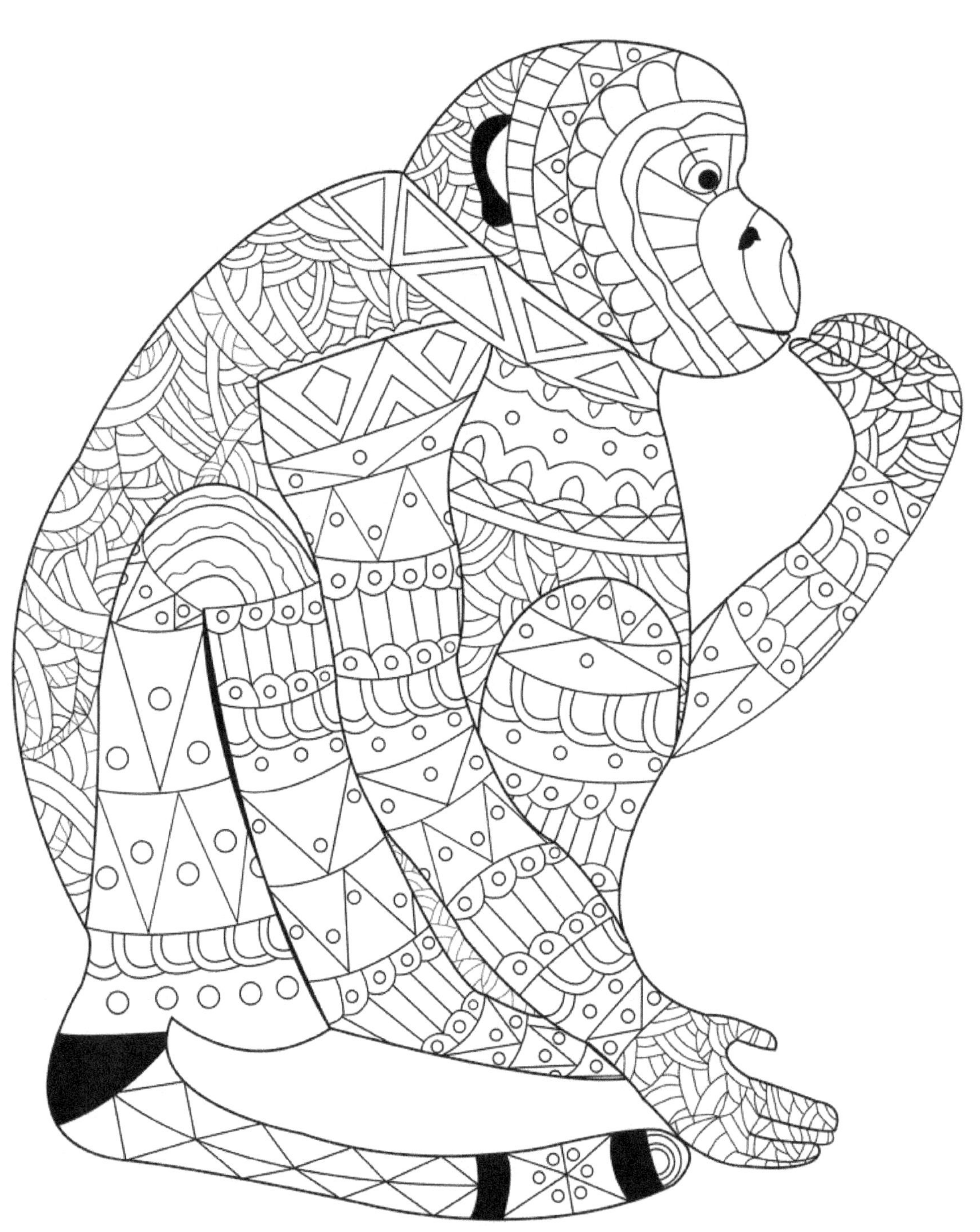

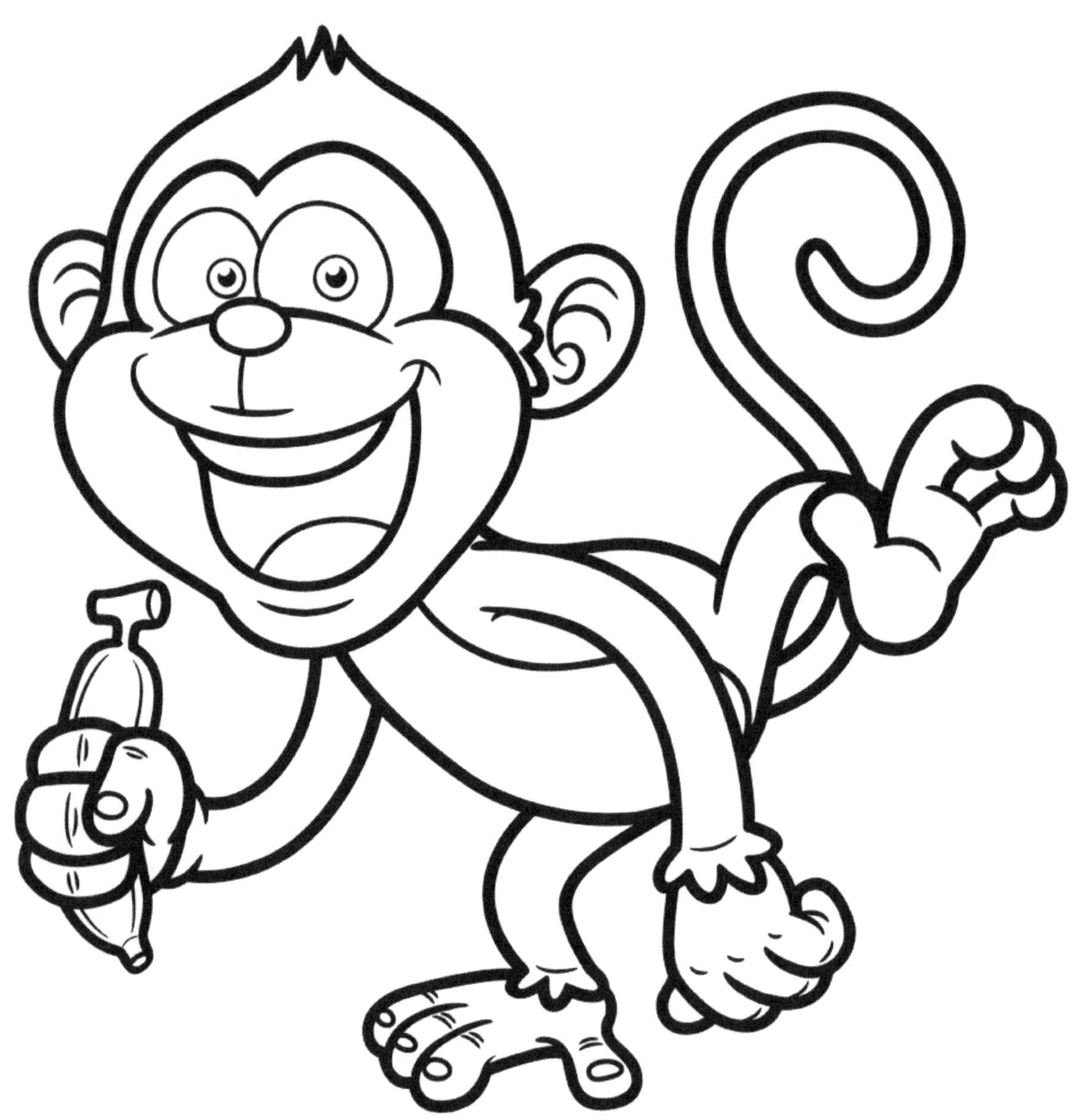

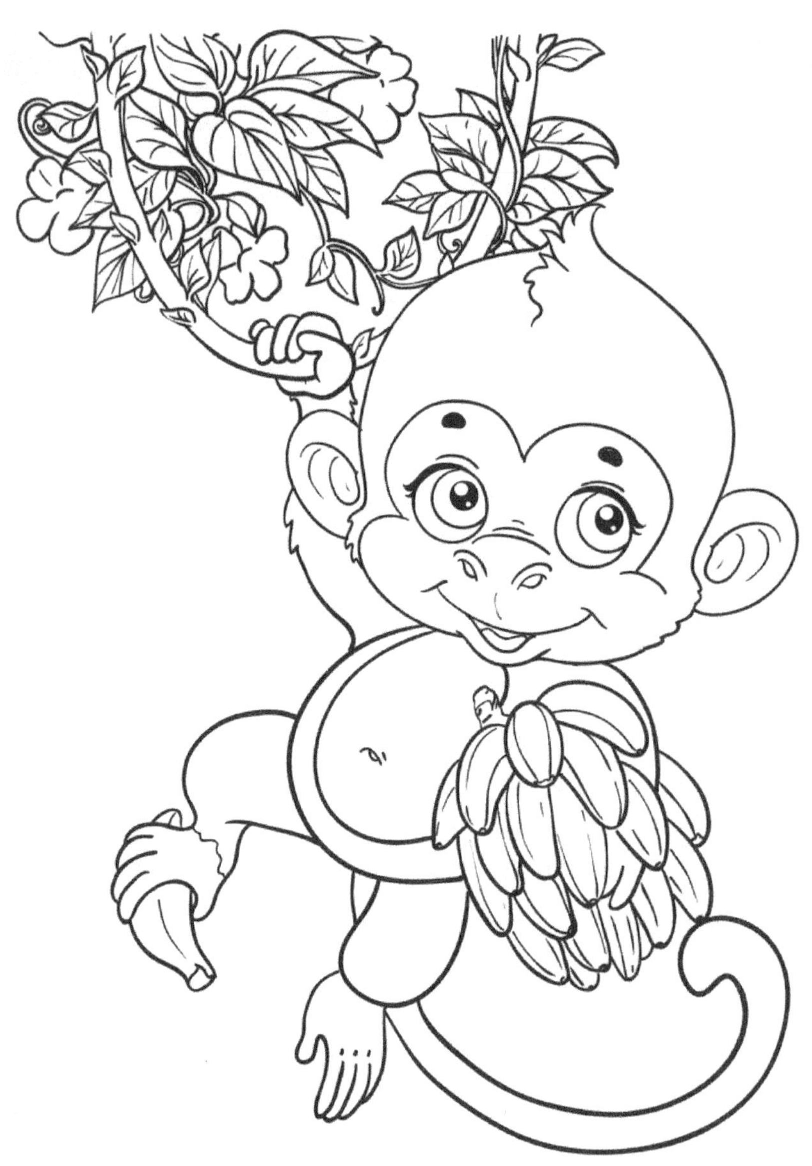

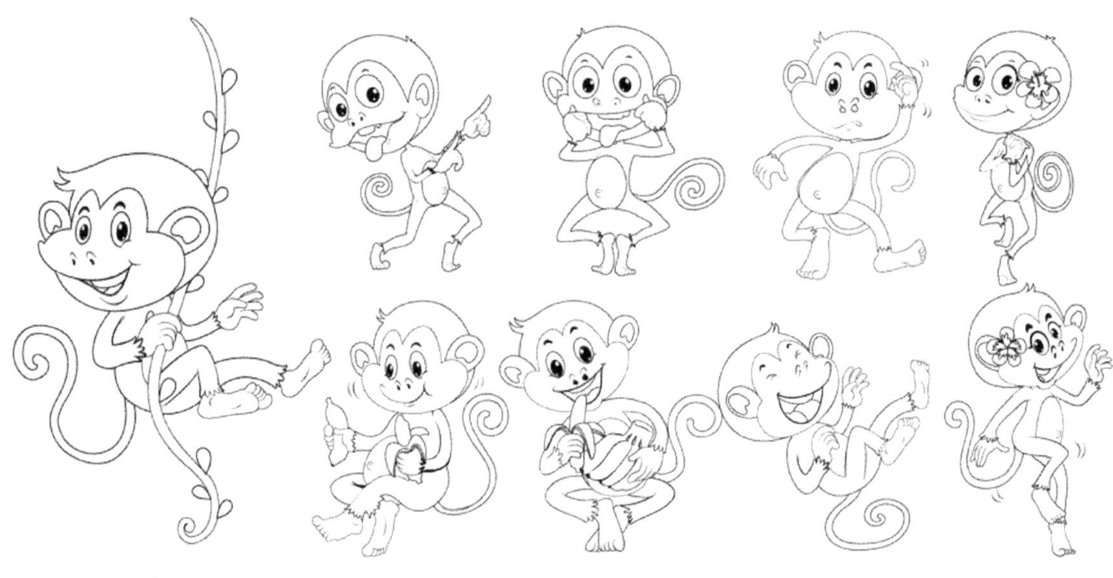

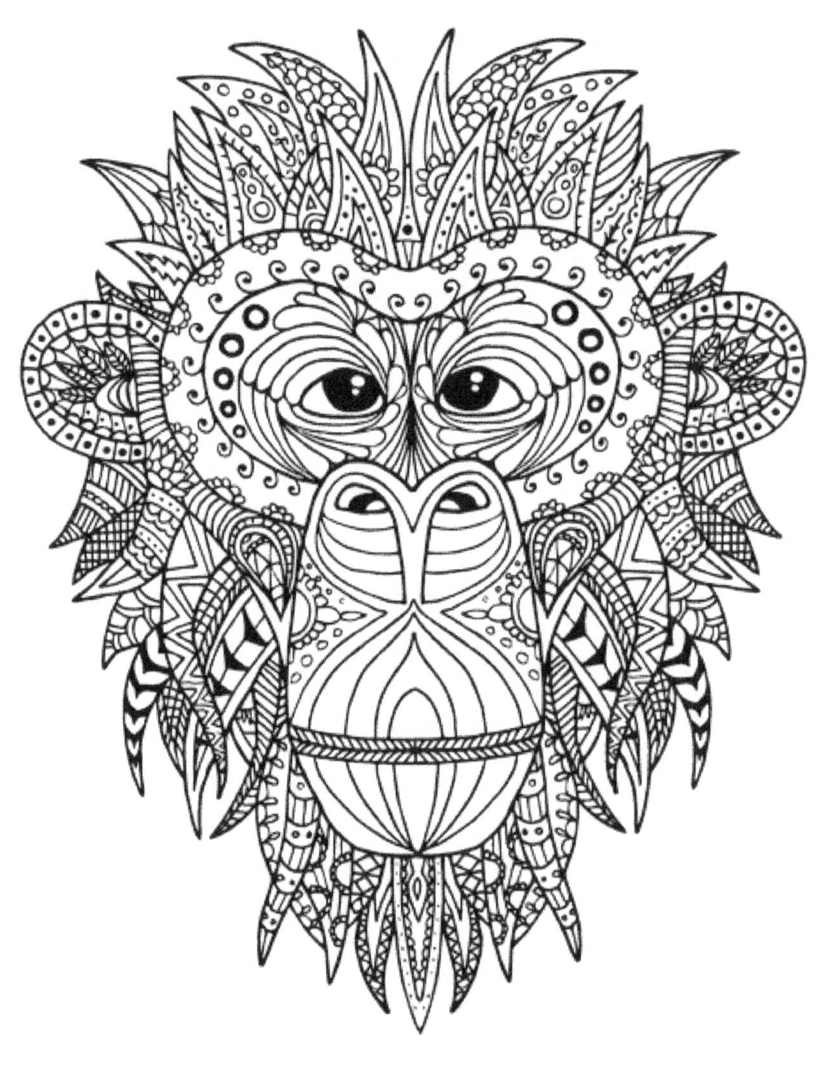

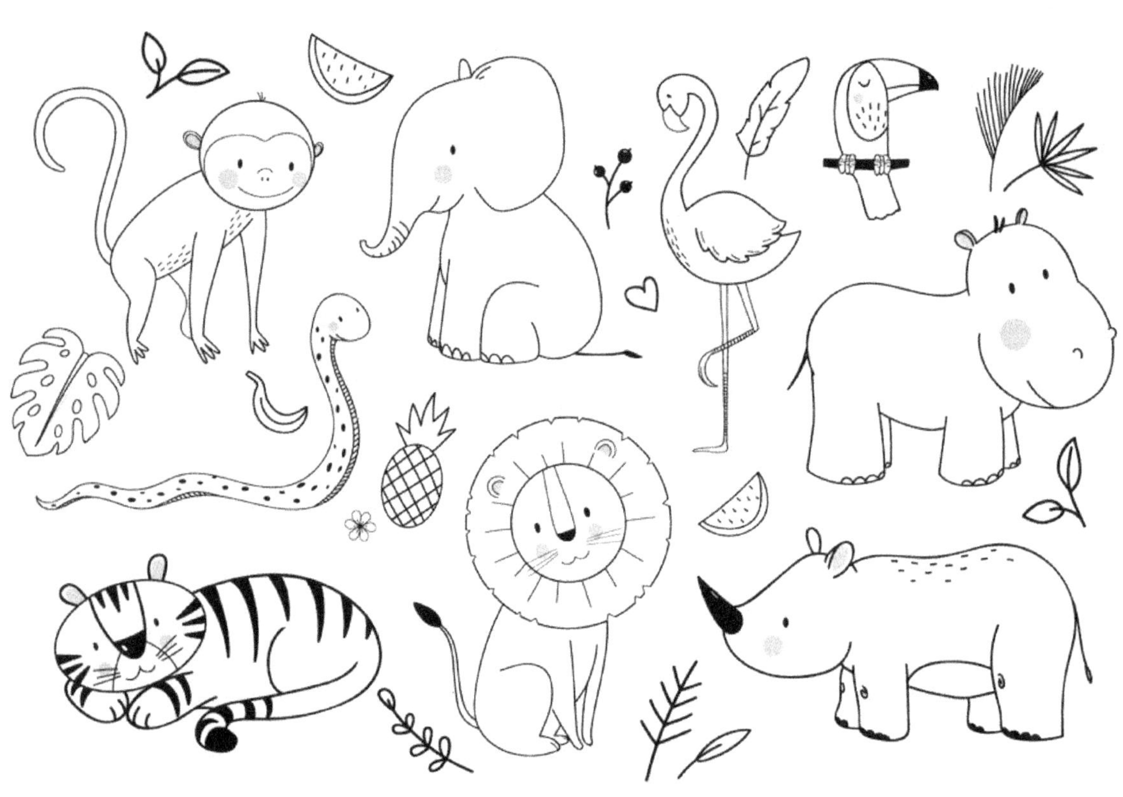

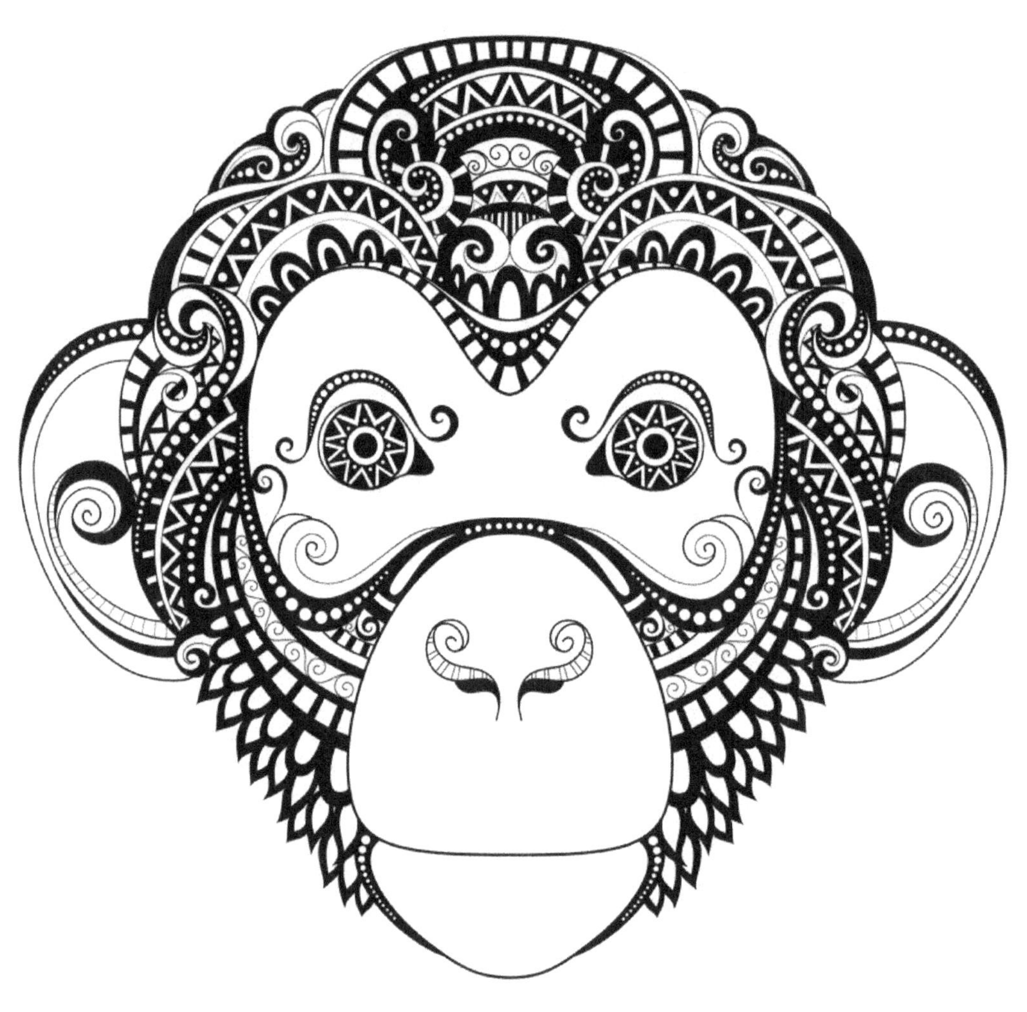

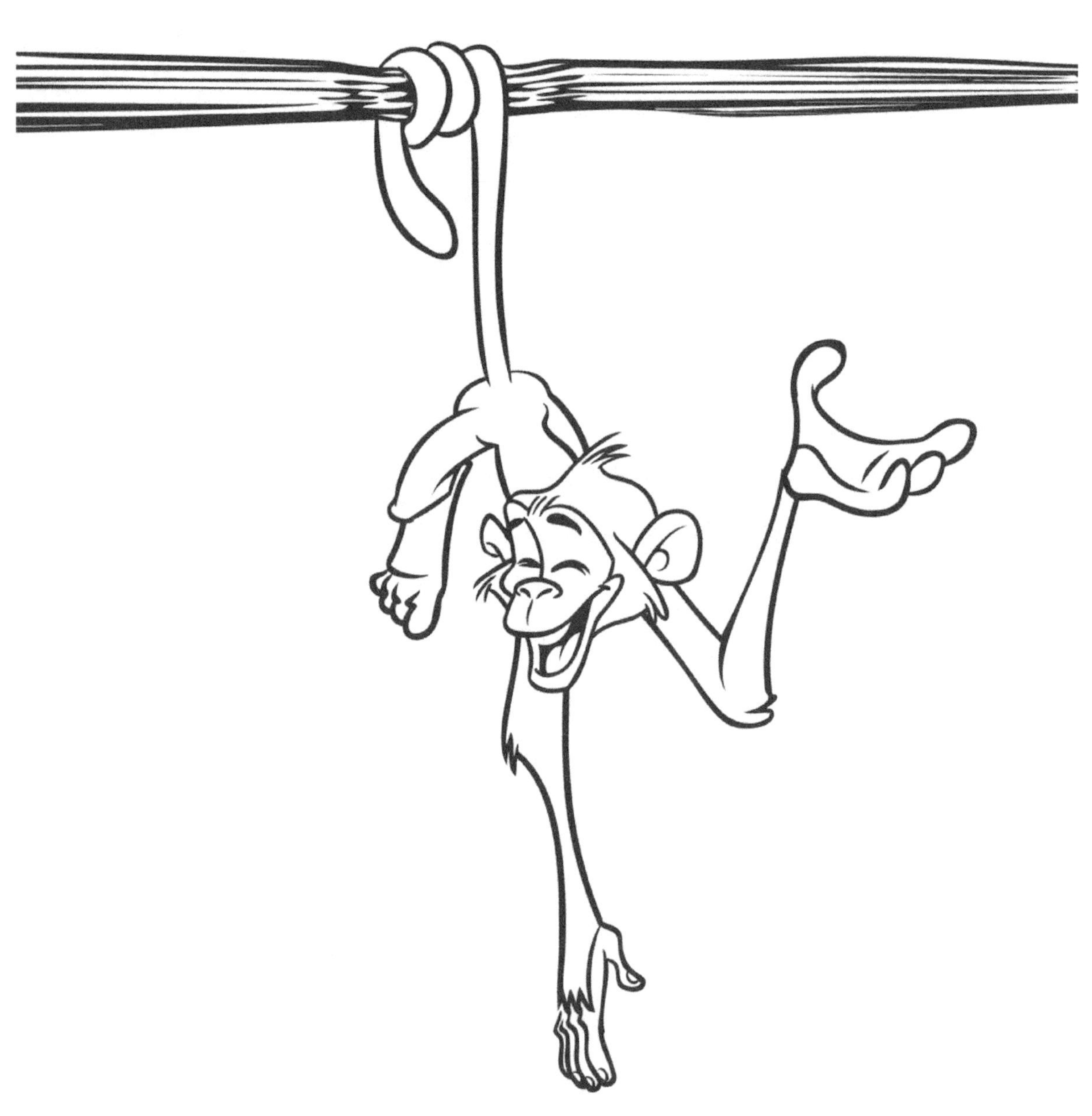

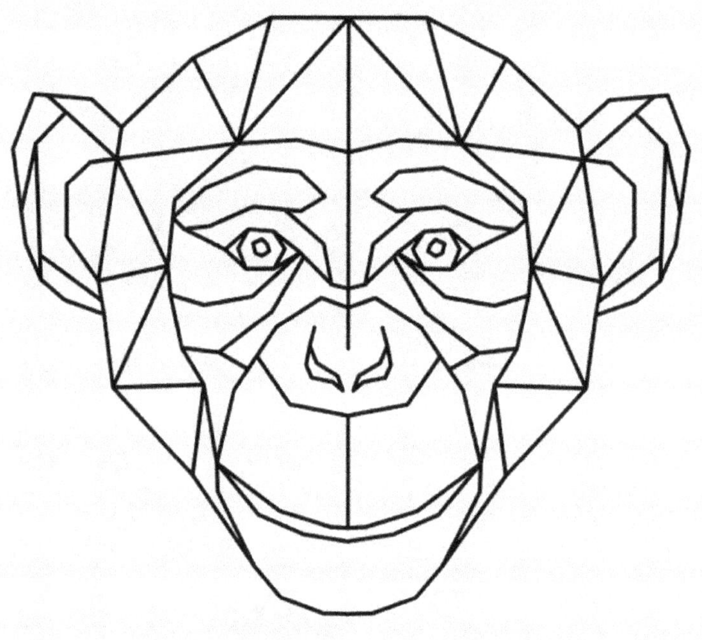

MONKEY

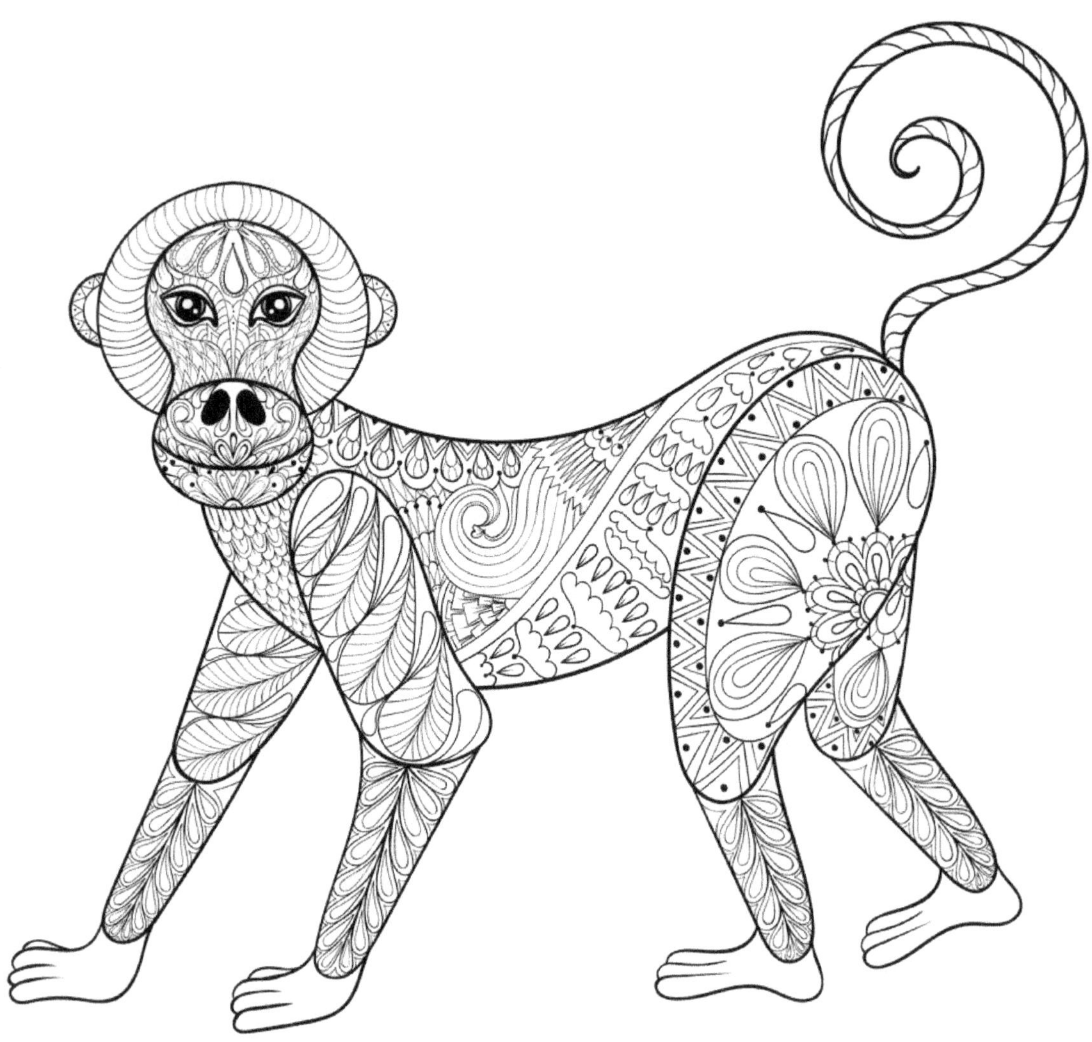

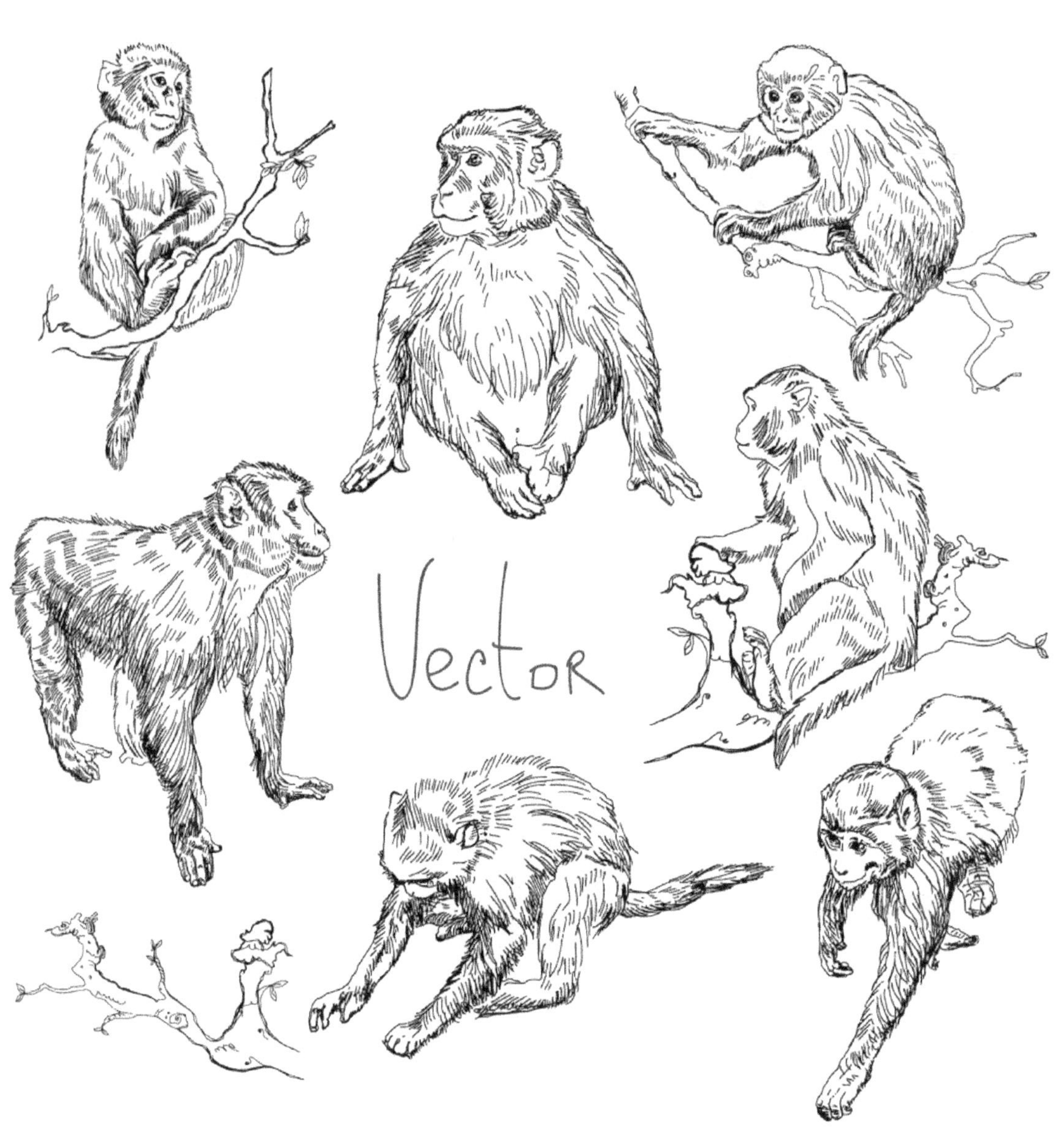

Vector

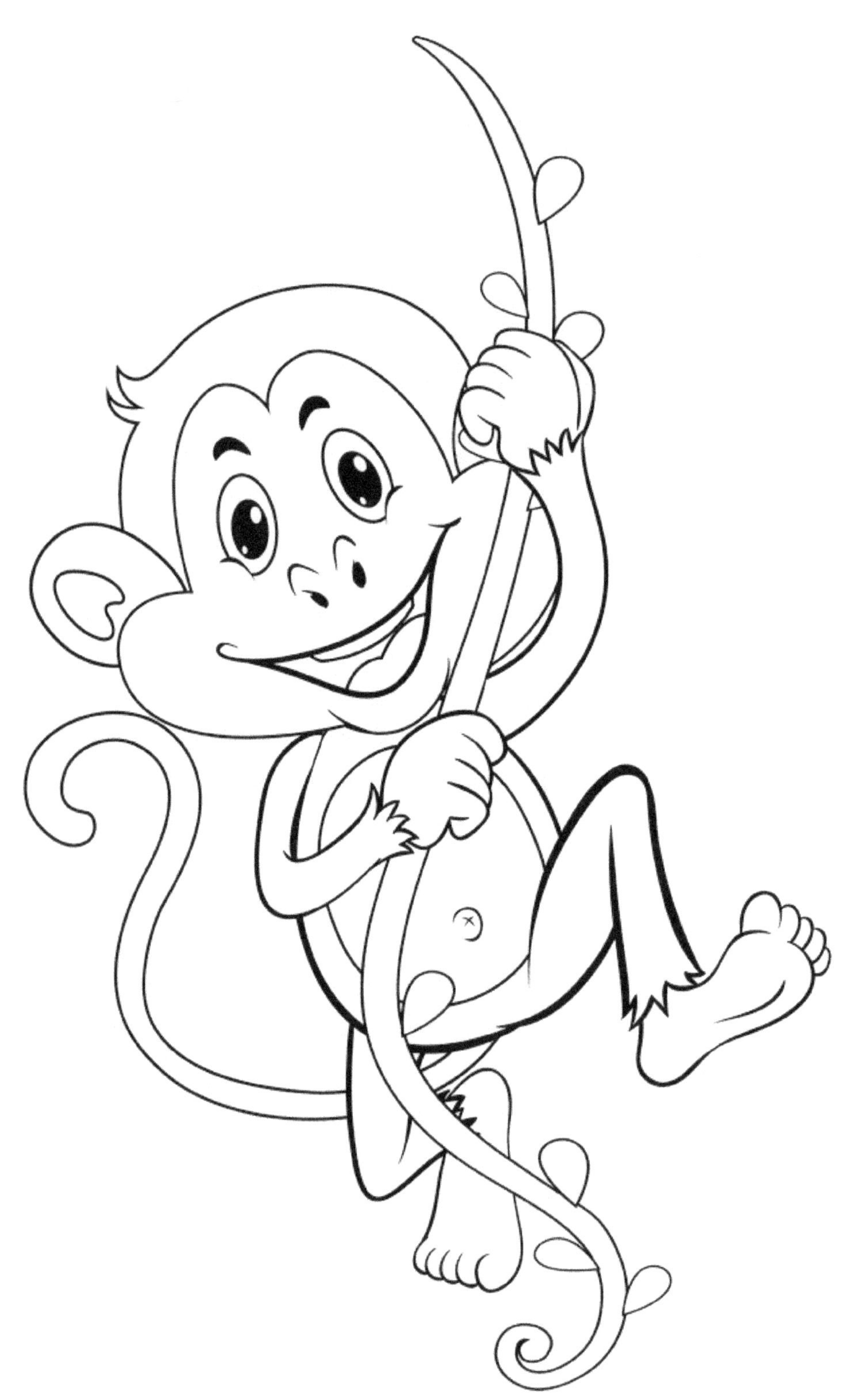

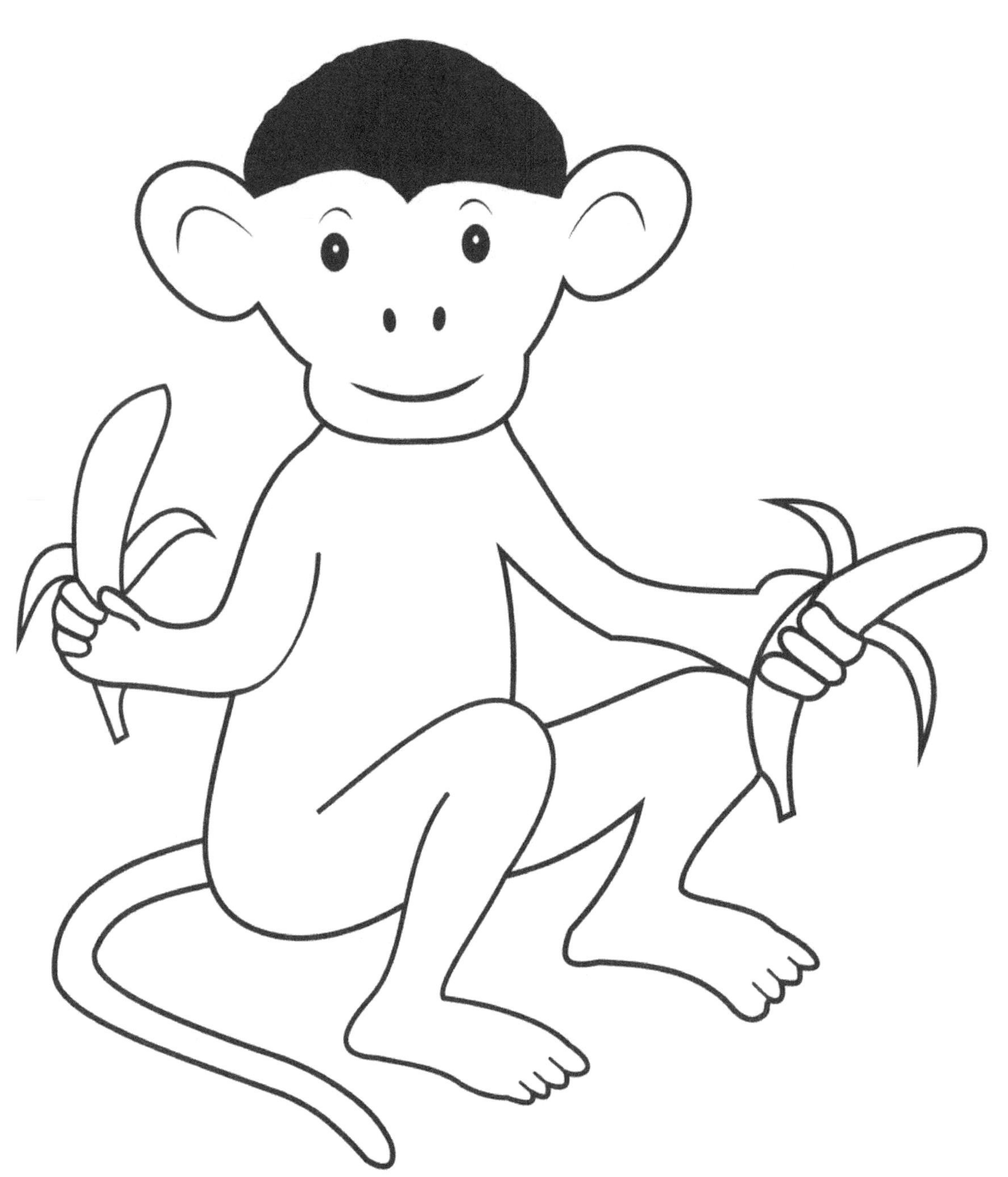

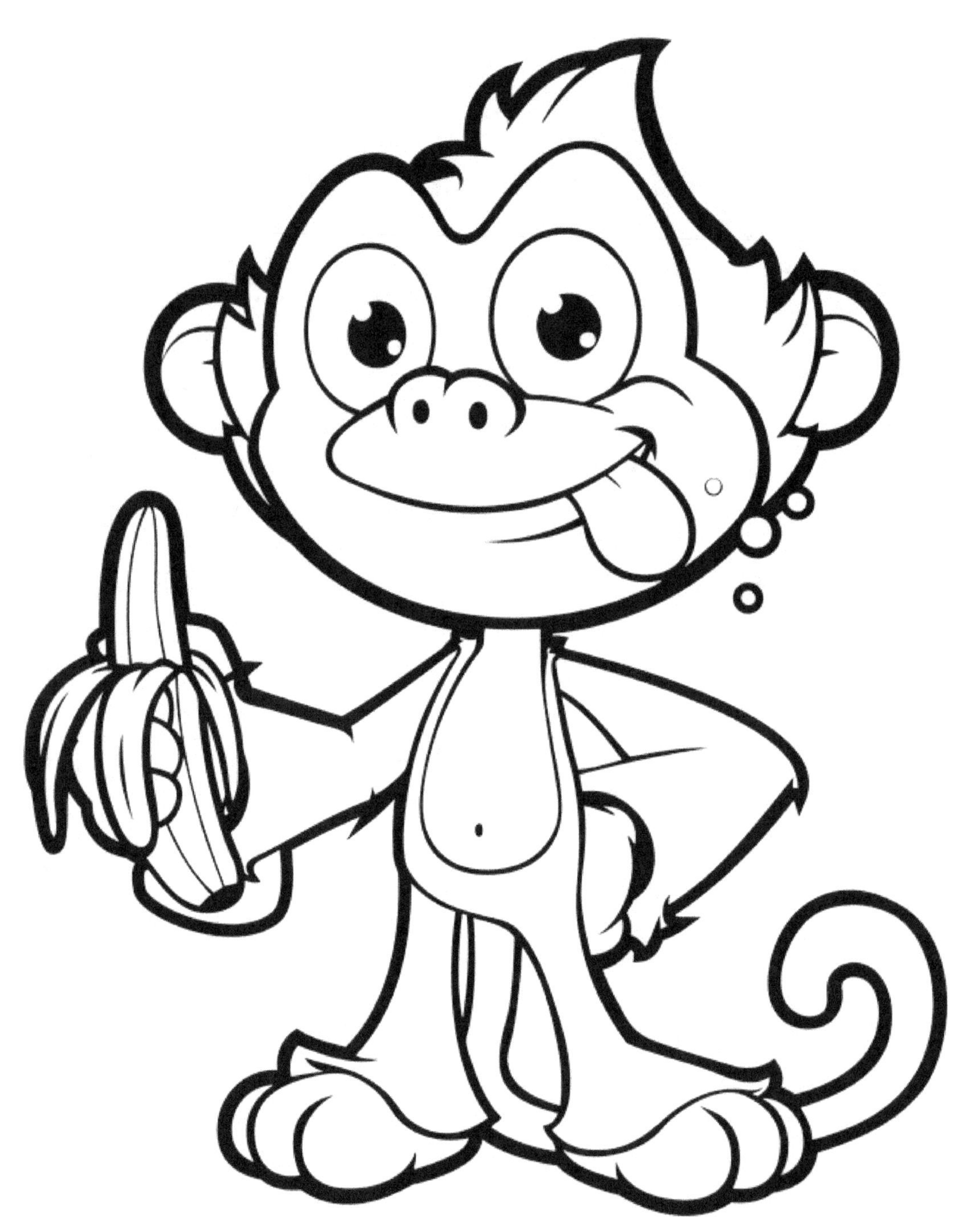

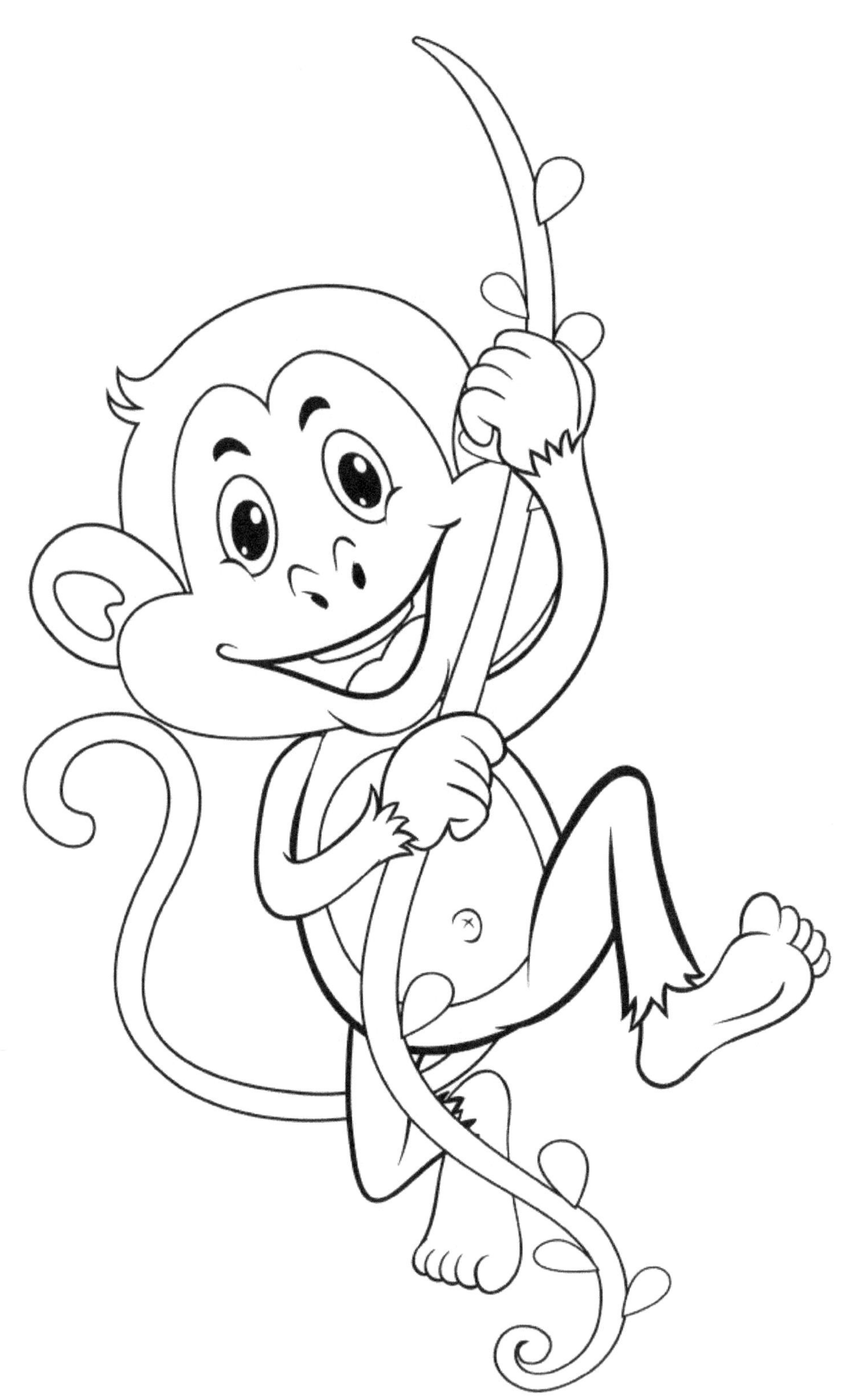

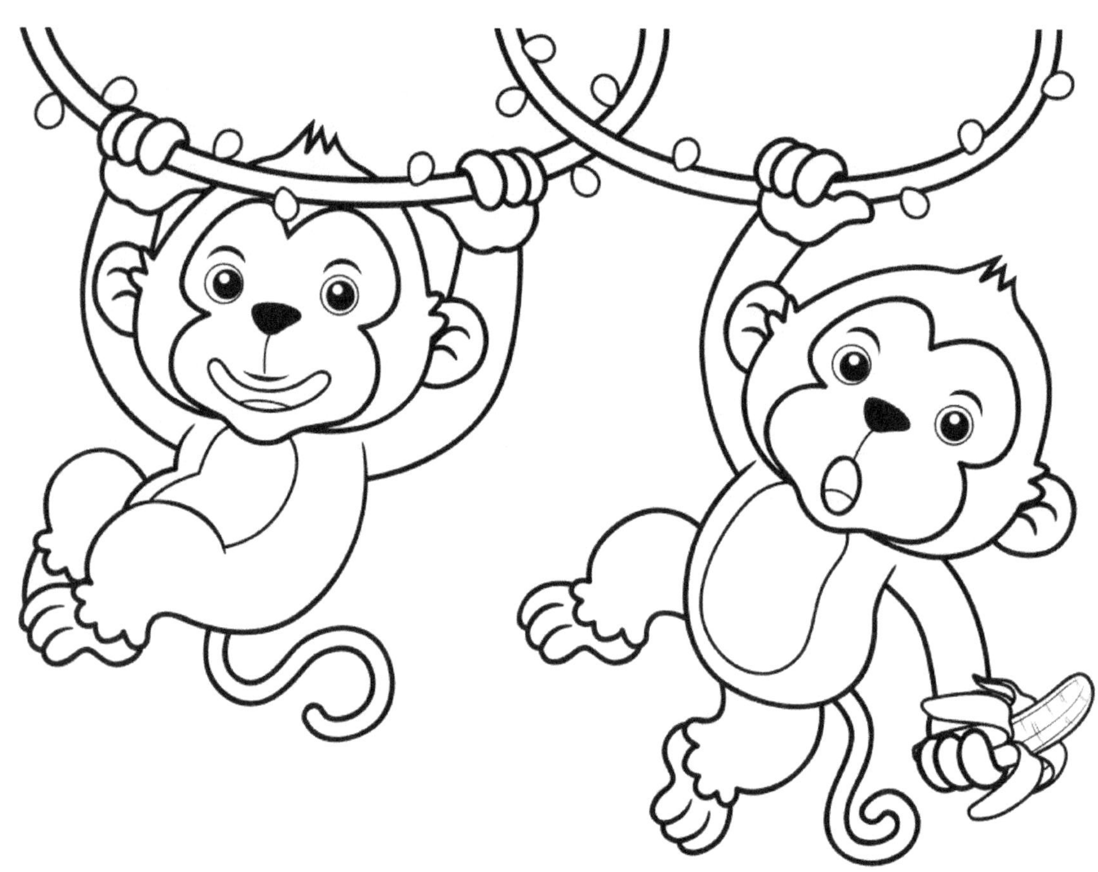

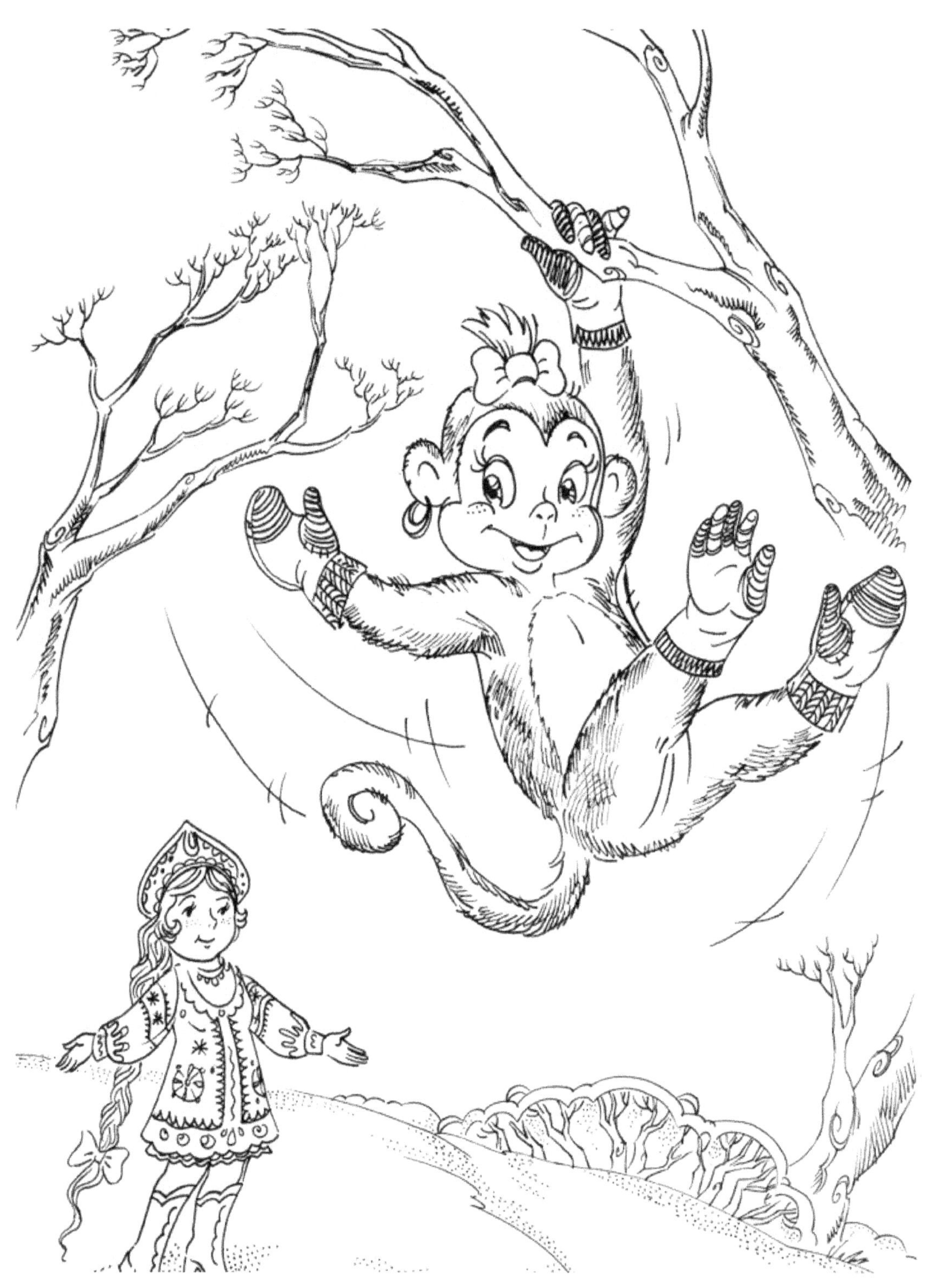

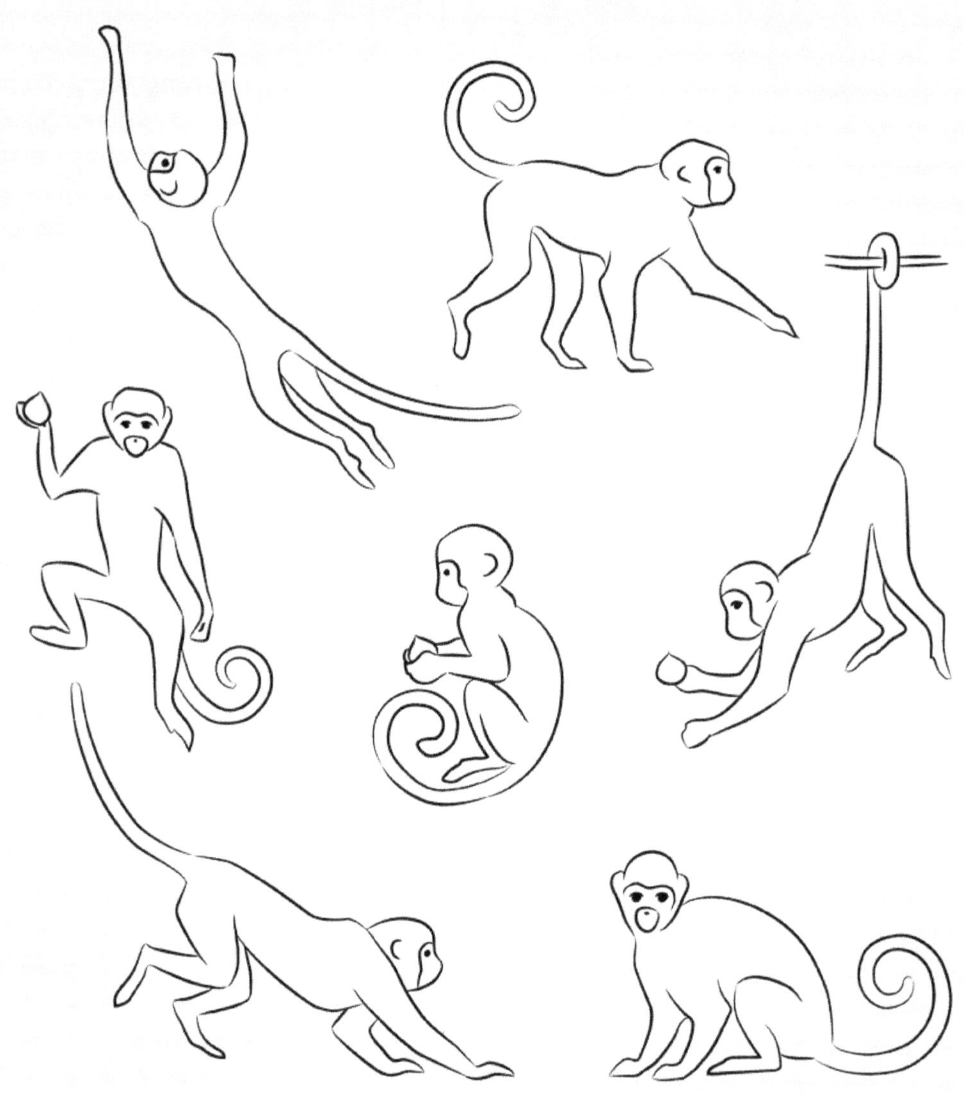

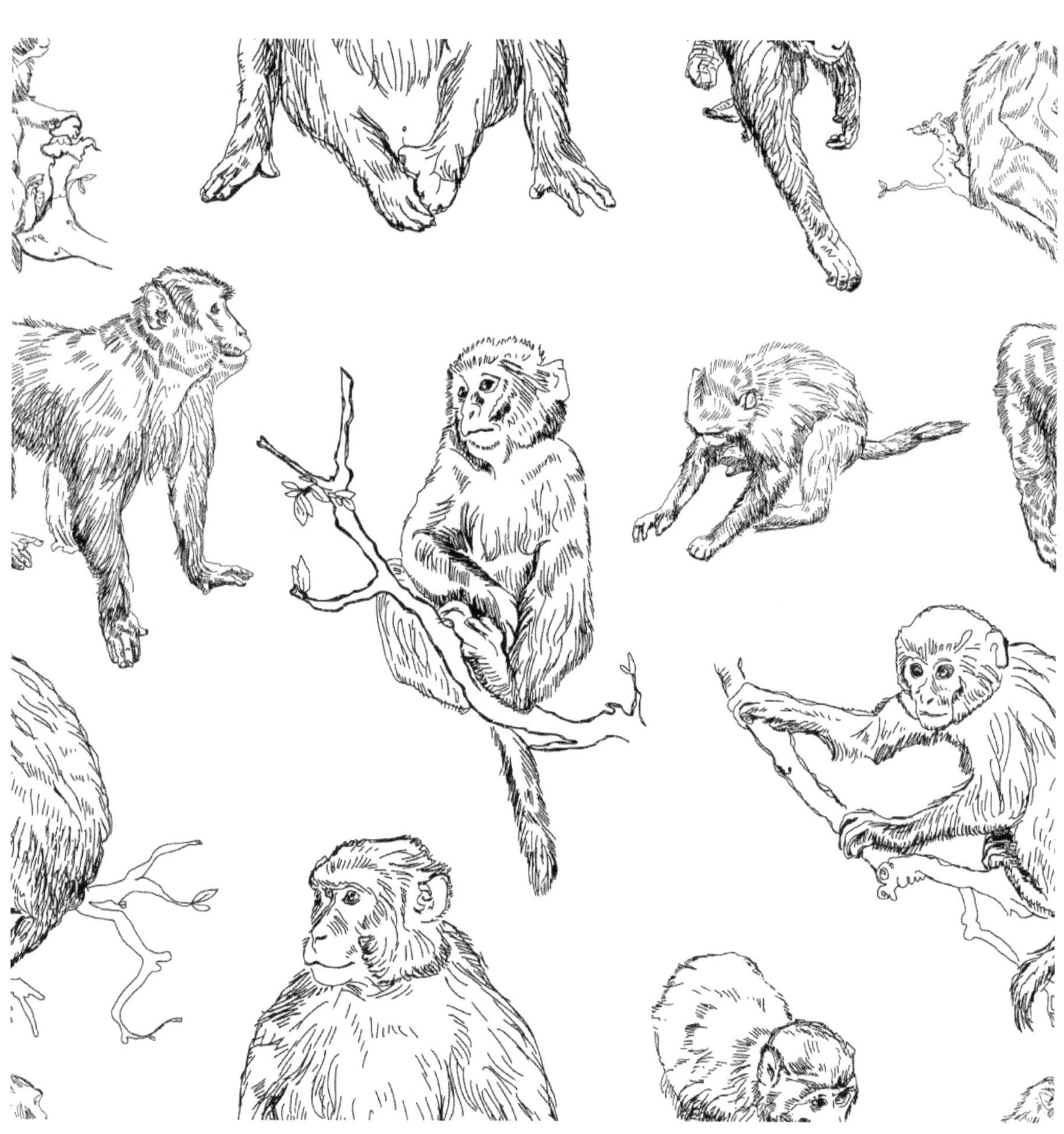

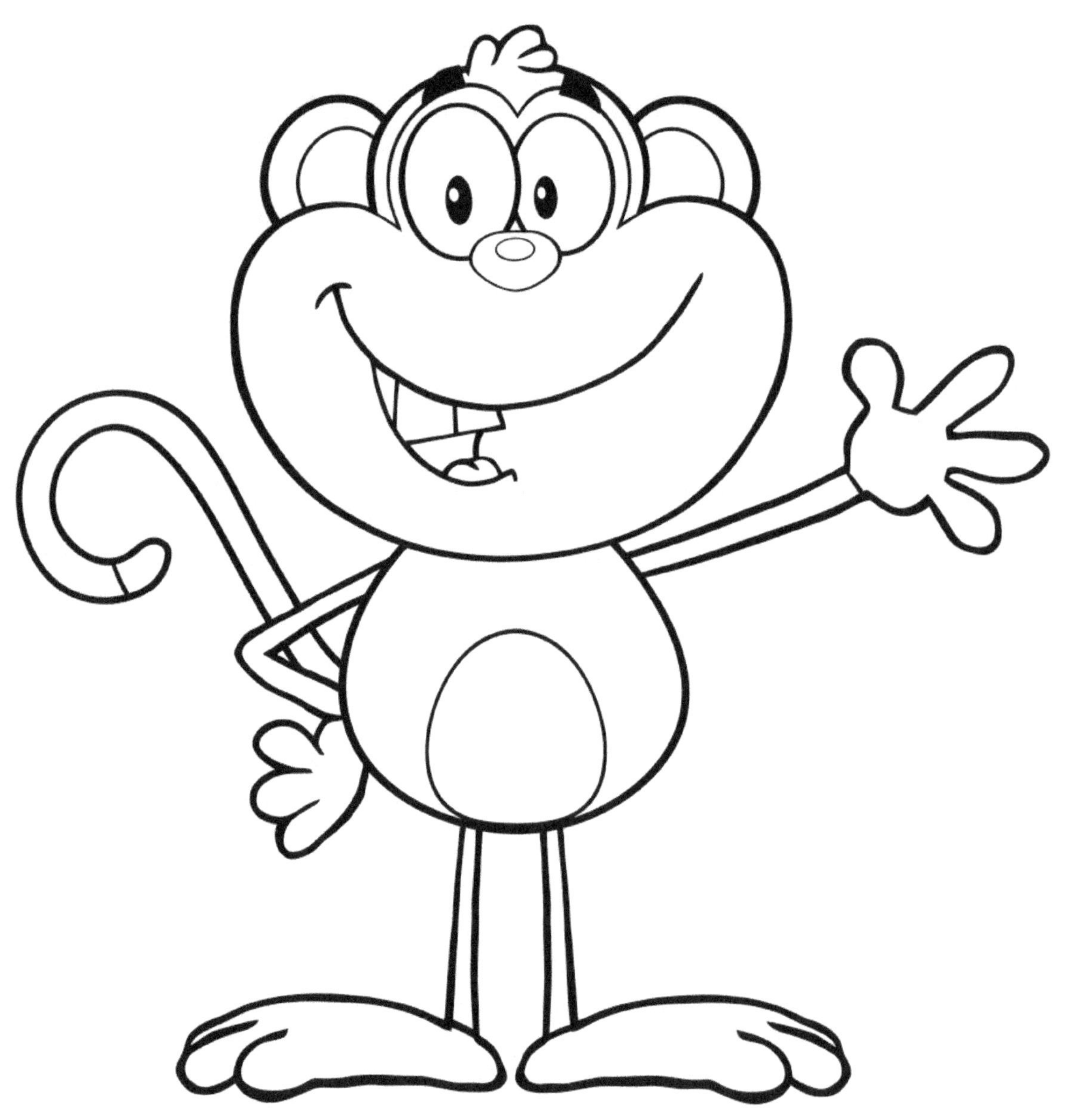

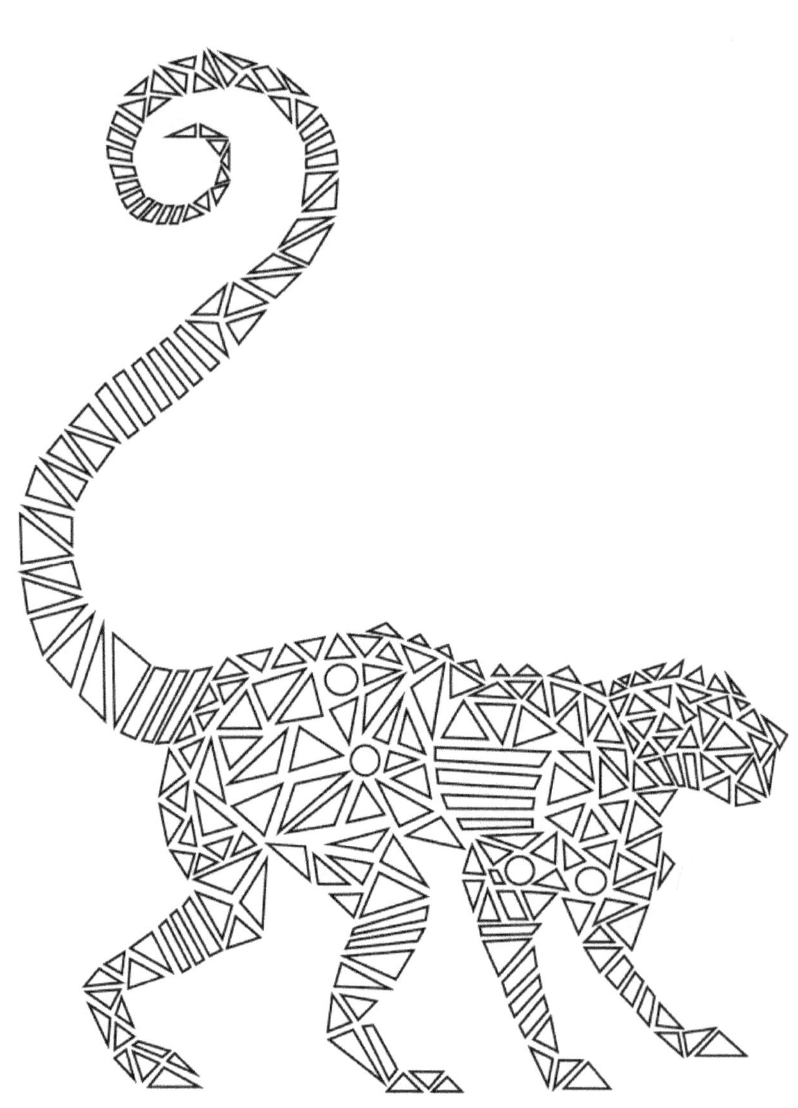

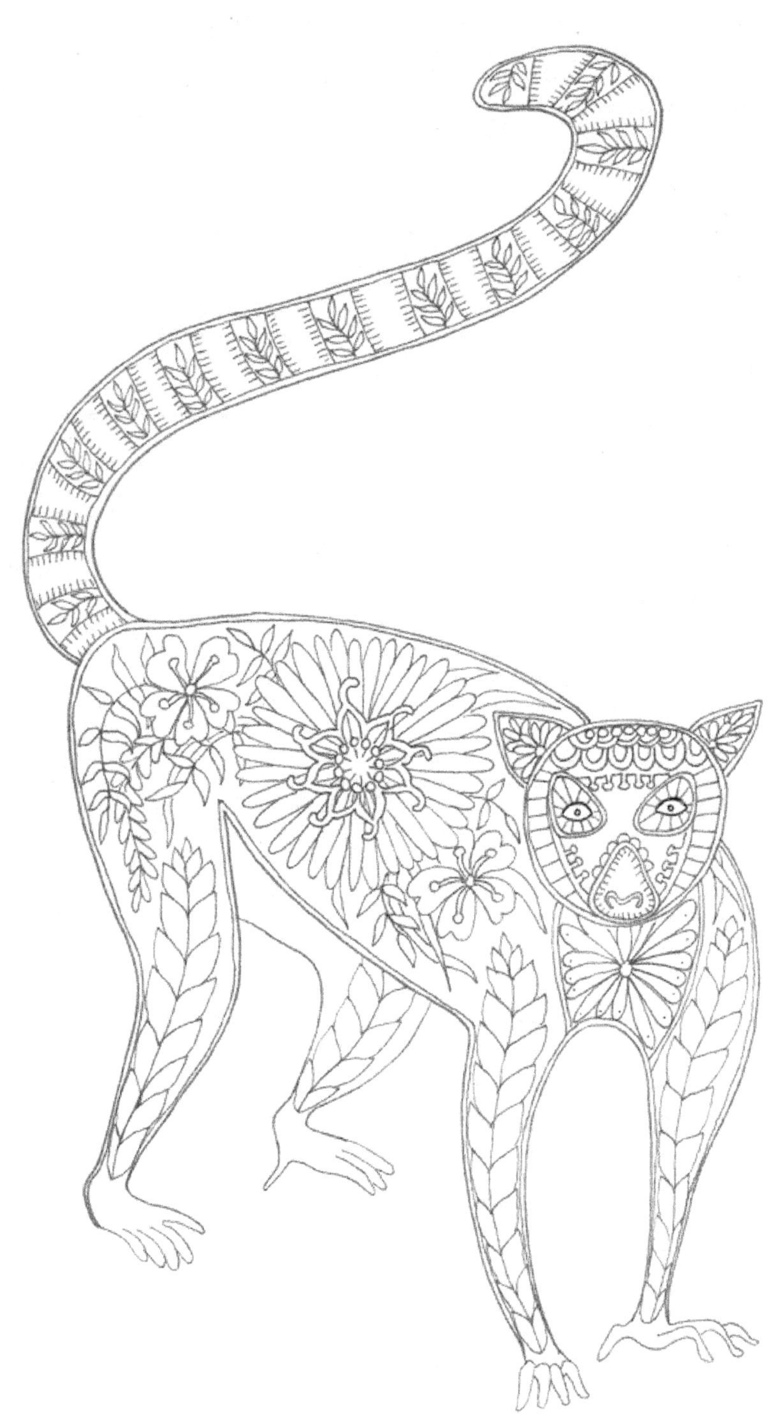